21.12.05

Communication, language and literacy

Planning and Assessment **Stepping Stones** **Early Learning Goals** **Practical activity ideas**

Jillian Harker

Goals *for the* Foundation Stage

British Library Cataloguing-in-Publication Data A catalogue record for this book is available from the British Library.

ISBN 0 439 98350 9

Author
Jillian Harker

Editor
Jane Bishop

Designer
Clare Brewer

Assistant Editor
Saveria Mezzana

Illustrations
Mary Hall

Series Designer
Clare Brewer

Cover photography
Derek Cooknell

Text © 2003 Jillian Harker
© 2003 Scholastic Ltd

Designed using Adobe Pagemaker

Published by Scholastic Ltd,
Villiers House,
Clarendon Avenue,
Leamington Spa,
Warwickshire CV32 5PR

Visit our website at www.scholastic.co.uk
Printed by Proost NV, Belgium

2 3 4 5 6 7 8 9 0   4 5 6 7 8 9 0 1 2

Acknowledgements
Qualifications and Curriculum Authority for the use of extracts from the QCA/DfEE document *Curriculum Guidance for the Foundation Stage* © 2000 Qualifications and Curriculum Authority.
Every effort has been made to trace copyright holders and the publishers apologise for any inadvertent omissions.

Communication, language and literacy

Contents

Communication, language and literacy

Chapter 5 Writing

Chapter 6 Handwriting

Photocopiable pages

Introduction

The books in this series aim to provide early years practitioners with support in planning, assessing and teaching the early years curriculum, as it is outlined in the document *Curriculum Guidance for the Foundation Stage* (QCA). This book helps to translate the guidance into ideas that will enable practitioners to target the Goals for Communication, language and literacy effectively and thoroughly. The activities suggested can be applied equally well to the documents on pre-school education published for Scotland, Wales and Northern Ireland.

The guidance specifies six clusters of Goals in this Area of Learning, two of which focus on the language skills needed for the purpose of communication and thinking. A third cluster targets children's ability to link sounds and letters, which provides a transition to the more formal skills of the remaining three clusters for reading, writing and handwriting.

Developing language

The close link between spoken language and the acquisition of early literacy skills has been well researched and is well documented. Young children need the opportunity to develop good spoken language skills in order to provide a solid foundation for the teaching of the more formal skills of reading and writing. Where a child's grasp of these underlying language skills is insecure, they are likely to experience problems in the acquisition of literacy.

To assist the children in reaching the Goals for Communication, language and literacy, your aim is to encourage them to communicate their feelings, ideas and thoughts with both their peers and adults. To achieve this, you will need to provide an environment in which they can share a wide range of stories, rhymes and books and in which language skills are linked with other Areas of Learning. You will also need to foster understanding of the alternative methods of communication that some children utilise, given their special needs, and you should aim to provide good models for language, reading and writing skills.

As language skills lie at the heart of the learning process, it is no exaggeration to say that they form the foundation on which all future learning is based. Language is the primary tool that we use for learning throughout our lives and competence in language enables each individual to play a full role in society. For this reason, the best early years settings will provide an environment in which children are encouraged to both listen and talk, and in which their verbal contributions to conversation, discussion and storytelling, as well as their questions about their world, are highly valued.

How to use this book

This book aims to support early years practitioners in providing a literate environment. It offers ideas for a wide range of activities that will help young children to develop the language skills that they need to further their learning. It also contains suggestions for activities that build on those language skills, to help the children to take the first important steps towards literacy.

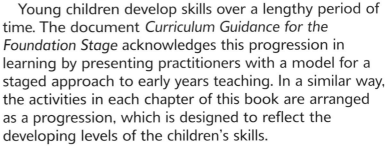

Young children develop skills over a lengthy period of time. The document *Curriculum Guidance for the Foundation Stage* acknowledges this progression in learning by presenting practitioners with a model for a staged approach to early years teaching. In a similar way, the activities in each chapter of this book are arranged as a progression, which is designed to reflect the developing levels of the children's skills.

In each chapter, the early activities target more basic skills while the activities in the latter part of each chapter will require some of those basic skills to be in place. This progression of activities may be useful in assisting your planning, enabling you to select suitable activities to work towards short- and long-term goals. The Stepping Stones for each activity have been colour-coded with activities at the simplest level shaded yellow, those in the middle shaded blue and the more difficult shaded green, to match the colours used to show progression in the *Curriculum Guidance for the Foundation Stage*.

However, since all activities include suggestions for extension for older children and support for younger children, use of the activities remains completely flexible.

Using the activities

Each activity is presented in an easily accessible form that makes it immediately clear which resources are required and how many children are best suited for that activity. Although a range of group sizes is suggested throughout the book, for many activities small groups are recommended. This does not mean that the activities cannot be carried out with larger numbers, but rather that smaller groups, or more helpers, are likely to prove more effective. Spoken language skills, for example, are more easily fostered in small group settings, rather than in larger groups, which might prove daunting for a young child. Moreover, small group work also allows for much more effective, ongoing monitoring at this crucial early stage of education.

Where preparation is necessary to carry out an activity, this is clearly indicated. Step-by-step instructions for successful completion of the activity are then provided and may include suggestions for modelling specific skills for the children, or for appropriate phraseology to use when introducing or carrying out an activity. Children who are given the opportunity to hear adults use language to reason, explain and question, and to watch adults reading and writing, should be encouraged to imitate the behaviour. The last two statements within each 'What to do' section offer ways to simplify the idea to support younger children, and to extend it for older children.

Following each main activity, 'More ideas' provides alternative suggestions which target the same Stepping Stone, and 'Other curriculum areas' shows how the same Stepping Stones and Early Learning Goals can be achieved across other Areas of Learning. These are identified in the shortened form of PSED (Personal, social and emotional development), CLL (Communication, language and literacy), MD (Mathematical development), KUW (Knowledge and understanding of the world), PD (Physical development) and CD (Creative development) to match the six Areas of Learning. 'Home links' offers advice on how to help the children to continue their learning at home with their parents and carers.

Photocopiable resources

Some activities are supported by photocopiable activity sheets (pages 83–96). These provide materials such as a resource for a play activity, a set of cards for a game and sheets for individual children to record their responses. The majority of the sheets are designed to allow the children to record a response without the need for formal writing skills. Where writing skills are needed, suggestions are included as to how to support any children who have not yet fully mastered the necessary skills.

The instructions for each activity clearly indicate how many copies of the photocopiable sheets need to be made in advance and whether these should be made on card to provide a more long-lasting resource. You may find it useful to laminate cards to be used for games in order to extend their usability.

Promoting learning

Young children learn best when they are using all their senses. They are active learners who explore the world around them through sight, touch, hearing, smell and taste. To capitalise on this multi-sensory learning, most activities in this book are based around concrete objects or a visual stimulus, such as picture cards or a book. Where books are suggested for storytelling, as an introduction to an activity,

suggestions for making this an interactive process are also given. As the children become aware that they are likely to be asked to respond to books, and that their responses will be listened to and valued, their attention and listening skills will be reinforced. Such skills are themselves prerequisites for the acquisition of spoken language skills.

Since much early learning is rooted in play, many of the suggested activities are based in play environments or use books as a stimulus for play scenarios. Purposeful play provides an opportunity to practise a range of skills. In acting out play scenarios, for example, the children can be encouraged to rehearse not only their verbal skills, but also emergent reading and writing skills. The planning section of this book contains additional ideas for creating a literate environment to maximise the opportunities that play provides.

Across all Areas of Learning

Young children do not compartmentalise their learning, and although the early years curriculum has been organised into six Areas of Learning, it is important to understand that these Areas will overlap or interlink. An activity that is designed to develop language skills may also involve the use of physical skills, or may, simultaneously, enhance a child's social skills. The ability to respond to favourite songs and rhymes, for example, might indicate that a child has mastered a Stepping Stone not only in the Area of Communication, language and literacy but also in the Area of Creative development.

The structure of this book helps to reinforce these links between the various curriculum areas, with additional suggestions for targeting the relevant Stepping Stone through an activity in another curriculum area provided in 'Other curriculum areas'.

Support from home

Learning becomes most effective when children are encouraged to practise skills in a variety of different settings. Each activity includes a 'Home links' suggestion that can be passed on to parents and carers to help them to support their children's learning. It is particularly important in the Area of Communication, language and literacy for carers to understand the enormous contribution that they can make simply by listening to their children, and by encouraging them to talk and ask questions. The impact that carers have on their children's learning can also be enhanced by explaining the positive benefits of modelling reading and writing behaviour.

Helping children to learn

As basic skills often develop interdependently, some activities in this book are cross-referenced. An item that children have constructed as part of one activity may serve a useful role as a prop for another play activity. An outing undertaken for the purpose of encouraging the children to explore the environment, and to hunt out relevant information afterwards, may also serve as an ideal stimulus to retell or record experiences.

Young children learn best of all in an atmosphere that is relaxed and enjoyable. When adults participate enthusiastically in their play and share the pleasure of conversation and of books, and when they provide models of spoken and written language skills, there is likely to be a huge incentive for the children to imitate that behaviour themselves. Where praise and encouragement form part of the daily experience, young children will be inclined to listen, respond, question, discuss and want to read and write. In such an environment, they stand the best possible chance of being able to learn.

Planning

Good planning plays a key role in enabling effective learning. By thinking and talking about children's learning, and how best to promote it, practitioners will be stimulated to create an environment that both supports and challenges children in the learning process. Good planning helps practitioners to make that learning process exciting, varied and progressive. It promotes the practitioners' understanding of how individual children learn and make progress.

Written plans

Practitioners will vary in their use of written plans. These may not always be essential but they can prove useful as a bank of significant information that can easily be shared with other people and be used for future reference and in future planning. They also provide a record of children's previous experiences and interests and, together with assessment information, can contribute towards an ongoing record of each child's progress. To be of optimum use, written plans need to be clear, concise and easy to complete.

Long-term plans

Long-term plans provide an overview of learning opportunities for up to a year ahead. Such long-term planning is important since a number of children may spend several years in the same setting. A long-term plan, which is usually designed with groups of children in mind, will therefore help to ensure that each child has a broad and balanced curriculum, with all six Areas of Learning given equal emphasis, over the period that they spend in the setting. An effective long-term plan will indicate when, and how frequently, various Areas of Learning will be taught, and how various aspects of learning will be linked in a way that is relevant and interesting for the children. It will also include any special events, such as visits, that will enhance a particular aspect of learning.

Short-term plans

Short-term plans are usually drawn up on a daily or weekly basis, and are designed with either groups of children or individual children in mind. It should be possible to adjust short-term plans to take account of any particular opportunities that occur to enhance learning. These would include unforeseen events or opportunities that arise as a result of the children's responses to the learning situation. It is particularly important to allow flexibility in short-term plans in order to be able to capitalise on any activity initiated by the children.

Communication, language and literacy

Using this book

The activities in this book are structured and set out in such a way as to provide support in effective long- and short-term planning. As each chapter contains a progression of ideas from beginning through to the end of the Foundation Stage, the later activities in any chapter can be used to inform longer-term planning, reflecting, as they do, more complex skills. Earlier activities in each chapter, on the other hand, might be used in shorter-term planning, enabling the children to move in a steady progression towards the Early Learning Goals for this Area of Learning.

The detailed information given for each activity regarding resources, preparation and group sizes will facilitate day-to-day or week-to-week planning. In addition, many of the play activities in this book can be viewed as open-ended, allowing you to extend the activity to reflect the children's responses and then to modify your short-term plans easily.

How to plan

Effective short-term planning is likely to be informed by ongoing observations of the children. At this level, planning and assessment interlink, as the monitoring of a child's progress will inform the planning of future learning steps. An understanding of the fact that children's development will vary both within and across the Areas of Learning, coupled with a good understanding of the Stepping Stones and Early Learning Goals, is of prime importance in enabling you to draw up effective short-term plans.

While written plans can be of considerable use, it is the process of planning which is of most importance. Since planning, observation and monitoring of children and assessing go hand in hand, the planning process is likely to be more effective, and easier, if key workers are assigned to groups of children. In this way, the information such workers glean from observation of specific children will flow easily back into the planning process.

Equal opportunities

Planning should take into account any special educational needs or disabilities that particular children have, indicating that reasonable adjustments have been made to ensure that disabled children, or those with special needs, are not placed at a disadvantage. Planning should take account of the children's experiences and should include a wide range of teaching strategies. The strategies suggested in the activities in this book are varied, and the multi-sensory approach used takes into account the differing learning styles of all children. Some of the support strategies suggested for younger children may also prove appropriate in helping children with special needs. In addition, you should always be prepared to make any other necessary adaptations. For example, you could supply a tape recorder to enable children who have particular difficulties in writing to record their observations, responses or story contributions. Some of the activities included in the book will also provide an opportunity to promote children's understanding of the special needs of other people.

Planning should also ensure equal opportunities for children of ethnic groups. The Communication, language and literacy Area of Learning offers many opportunities to capitalise on the learning possibilities provided by cultural diversity. Activities such as 'A special time' on page 27 create opportunities to explore each child's particular interests and can be used to plan for such coverage. Sensitive awareness should also inform the planning of any food-related activity when dietary requirements may need to be taken into account.

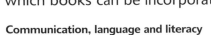

Take particular care to ensure that boys and girls alike have equal access to all play areas. Where planning is effective, girls will, for example, view construction toys as a natural resource for learning, and boys will frequently be found in the home corner, looking after a doll or pretending to do the washing-up. In such an environment, the language and communication development of all children will be enriched.

A literate environment
In planning for Communication, language and literacy, a primary concern must be to ensure that the learning environment maximises every opportunity to stimulate language development. Your goal should be to create a literate environment, one that is rich in print, and one in which children are encouraged to explore and experiment with both spoken language and print.

A book corner
Books will play a key role in creating a successful literate environment. In the reading area or book corner, aim to display some books with their front covers facing forwards. Consider providing photocopies of the front covers of books in current use, so that the children know where to replace a book when they have finished with it.

Provide a quiet, comfortable area near by, where the children can browse through and share books. By including a table and chairs in this area, you will make it possible for the children to study larger books more closely when they wish to seek out more detailed information.

Books everywhere
Books should not, however, be confined to one area. In the best settings, they will invade every part of the room. There are numerous ways in which books can be incorporated into a variety of activities.

© DIGITAL STOCK

Display books with numbers near to other number equipment, and add story-books to the home corner so that the children can read bedtime stories to dolls and teddies.

Books can also be used as a primary source to stimulate play, encouraging children to practise spoken language skills. Provide 'story sacks' (or boxes) with props alongside favourite story-books to enable the children to re-enact their favourite tales. One for 'Goldilocks and the Three Bears' (Traditional), for example, might contain three bowls, three cushions and three blankets of differing sizes to stimulate role-play. Some sacks might contain dressing-up clothes appropriate for a given story, others a set of puppets.

The best learning environments will display an understanding of the concept of a book in its broadest possible sense, promoting children's awareness of the multiple purposes for which we use reading. Place a telephone directory next to a play phone, recipe books near to the cooker, magazines and catalogues in the home corner, and DIY books as an appropriate and interesting addition to the construction area.

A writing corner

The tools and materials necessary for writing should also be readily accessible to all children. Set out an area devoted to writing, and provide the children with a range of paper and card in a variety of colours, shapes and sizes. Place pencils and pens within easy reach. It is important for young children to experiment with a variety of writing tools, so crayons, wax crayons, felt-tipped pens and charcoal would all be useful additions to this area. Include envelopes, paper clips and clipboards with pencils on

Communication, language and literacy

string to allow the children to carry writing activities over into other areas of the learning environment.

Site a group post-box near to the writing area and encourage the children to leave notes for one another or for their parents and carers. Invite carers to use the post-box too, to leave occasional notes for their children. By including parents and carers in such a way, you will also be forging invaluable links between the learning environment and home. Parents and carers will see good models of teaching and learning behaviour as they deliver and collect their children, and will be provided with the means to emulate this behaviour at home, using the ideas that they have seen provided.

Words all around

Just as it is important for books to invade the room, so, too, should materials for writing. These should be provided wherever there is the possibility of them being used purposefully in play. Diaries can be transformed into appointment books for hospital play, order forms will add realism to a play post office, and a pack of sticky notes placed by the telephone will allow the children to take down messages. The aim should be to give young children a sense of the many purposes for which we use writing in everyday life.

To further enhance learning, the litcrate environment will make maximum use of signs and posters, both those made by practitioners and those produced by the children themselves. Whenever possible, display print at the children's eye height.

A sign over the home corner might read 'Hospital' at one time and 'Three Bears Cottage' at another, reflecting current activities and the children's interests. A sit-and-ride vehicle might be given a temporary 'Ice cream' sign so that it can be incorporated into play at the sand-pit 'beach'. In this way, it becomes natural for the children to view print as conveying meaning.

Teaching writing skills

It is very important that children experiment with writing and with writing implements at this stage of development, but it is also essential that good habits be encouraged. While access to the writing area should be free and experimentation should be encouraged, it is equally important to teach the children certain things alongside the free use of this area. Left alone, young children can acquire poor writing habits, which will be more difficult to correct later.

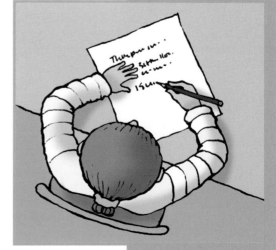

Posture and position

Plan to encourage correct writing posture, a good pencil hold and correct letter formation from the outset. In order to adopt an appropriate posture and to write comfortably, children need to be seated so that their feet rest flat on the floor. When their legs are too short to reach the floor, provide low boxes or cushions to place beneath their feet to stabilise them. The chair needs to be close enough to the table to support the child's back.

Planning

Explain to the children that writing is easier and less tiring, even for adults, if the writer sits in the correct position. The correct positioning of paper on the table also contributes to a good writing posture as shown in the diagram on page 13.

Holding the pencil
The use of a correct hold on the pencil or pen can mean the difference between writing becoming a fluid, easy process or a tiring, slow, sometimes painful one, which the child consequently tries to avoid. The correct hold uses three fingers, the forefinger and thumb being placed on either side of the writing tool, and the middle finger supporting the tool from beneath (see diagram). The fingers should be sited one to two centimetres from the tip of the pencil. Children vary in the speed with which they are able to adopt this grip, but they should have it modelled for them from the start and should be supported by the provision of appropriate writing implements.

Round, shiny pencils are the most difficult for young children to grasp; thicker triangular or faceted pencils with a matt finish often prove easier. Where children are finding it particularly difficult to hold a pencil correctly, provide rubber pencil grips to support them in achieving this.

Some young children experiment with using different hands for writing. If this is the case, observe the child to ascertain which hand is used more often and then encourage consistent use of that hand. No child should ever be forced to use a hand to write that is not their natural preference. Planning should take account of the particular needs of left-handers. Practitioners modelling letter formation for left-handed children should use their own left hand. The crossing strokes for the letters 't' and 'f' should be taught from right to left for these children. Fingers may need to be placed on the pencil slightly further away from the point than for a right-handed child. Appropriate left-handed tools such as scissors should be provided for activities other than writing.

Play areas and the role of practitioners
All play areas in an early years environment can be utilised to promote language, communication and literacy skills. As you engage with children in play activities, you will be modelling the language structures and vocabulary that the children need for learning. As you help the children to explore and discuss the feel of wet and dry sand, their vocabulary store will expand. As they weigh and measure toys in the play hospital, they will reinforce their mathematical language. As they question and experiment at the water trough, they are introduced to the language of science. Good planning should encourage practitioners to explore the full range of possibilities offered by every play area for the development of language, communication and literacy skills.

Communication, language and literacy

Assessment

Why assess?
Even coverage
Appropriate assessment can act as a check to reassure practitioners that they are providing truly effective coverage of all the Stepping Stones and Early Years Goals. Used well, ongoing monitoring of the children's progress should feed back into the planning process. It should inform the choice and pace of activities, both for groups of children and for particular individuals, indicating where changes may be needed, to ensure that the plans will meet the learning needs of all the children.

Useful communication
A second reason for assessing children and documenting their attainments, is to facilitate communication between practitioners within the Foundation Stage and those working in Key Stage 1. Important information can then be easily transferred from one practitioner to another, so that time is not wasted re-covering ground that a child has already covered. Transfer of relevant information can also help to prevent gaps from occurring in a child's learning. Assessment records can help to focus practitioners on areas of a child's learning that, for a variety of reasons, may need extra input.

Special needs
Good assessment practices should in addition provide practitioners with indications of any difficulties that children are experiencing, alerting them to the possibility of any special educational needs that those children may have. This aspect of assessment is particularly important as the earlier the child receives support for any special needs, the greater the chance of minimising any damage resulting from the difficulties. Where such needs are not appropriately addressed, the impact on the child's future learning and on their emotional well-being can be enormous. Assessment can therefore provide evidence of need for modification of learning activities. It may also provide crucial evidence that would be of help to support agencies on whose expertise you as the practitioner may wish to draw.

In addition, there may be children who have special educational needs that are not rooted in a particular difficulty, but on the contrary are the result of a particular strength or aptitude. Effective assessment will also alert you to these strengths, enabling you to plan future learning steps for these children in order to develop their strengths.

Communication, language and literacy

Assessment

Monitoring teaching methods

Finally, when assessment practices are carried out well, they enable you to reflect on your own practice. If the children are responding well to the activities on offer and progressing steadily through the various Stepping Stones, then it is likely that the breadth and level of those activities, and your approach, are appropriate for those children. If, on the other hand, assessments highlight certain areas as being less effective, you may wish not only to adjust your planning, but also to modify and refine your approach in the light of that evidence. In this respect, assessment contributes to your own professional development. In all respects, it should enhance the learning experience of the children.

© DEREK COOKNELL

How to carry out assessment

Assessment can be carried out on either an informal or a formal basis. Informal assessment is likely to be based on observations of the children as they carry out a range of activities. It will almost certainly take place over a period of time and will provide an ongoing record of a child's developing skills. The photocopiable sheets on pages 79–82 provide examples of an informal assessment procedure that cover the areas of speaking and listening, reading and writing.

Formal assessment, on the other hand, usually takes place at a given point in time and is conducted as a specific assessment activity, to check whether particular skills have been properly mastered by the children. The letter/sound checklist on page 18 provides an example for this kind of specific assessment.

In January 2003, the Qualifications and Curriculum Authority introduced a new assessment document for early years practitioners working within the Foundation Stage. The *Foundation Stage Profile* provides a 12-page document to be completed for each child throughout the Foundation Stage. Within it the curriculum is broken down to provide assessment for all six Areas of Learning, with 36 'targets' for Communication, language and literacy.

It is vital that children have a positive experience of any assessment procedure, in particular any formal assessment, which should be prefaced by a period of general conversation in order to put the child at ease. Explain the purpose of the assessment activity to the child in a positive way. For example, when you are checking a child's knowledge of letter sounds and names, you might say, 'I've noticed that you seem to know a lot more of your letters recently. Could we go through them, so that you can show me exactly which ones you do know?'.

Any recording marks that you make on record sheets should not be transparently obvious to the child. It is inadvisable to use ticks and crosses, for example, but slashes in different directions are an appropriate way to record correct and incorrect answers. Show sensitivity when a child reaches a point at which they are starting to struggle and cease your assessment, ending with a positive remark such as 'You've done really well. I think we'll stop there'. Likewise, formal assessment should cease at once if a child is exhibiting signs of stress.

Using the assessment sheets provided

Completion of the record sheets on pages 79–82 will most appropriately be carried out by someone who has the opportunity to observe a child over a period of several weeks. Many groups find it helpful to assign key workers to particular groups of children so that they have the opportunity to have a clear and full picture of each child's skills and interests.

A major role for key workers will be to carry out detailed observation of their group as the children engage in the learning activities. Allow the children to become familiar with the setting over a period of weeks before you complete the first assessment checklist. A second assessment half-way through the year will allow sufficient time for skills to have developed, or for any modification to the learning programme to have taken effect. A final opportunity for assessment should be taken at the end of the year.

Since the development of children's skills is gradual, and may include plateaux or setbacks, it is inadvisable to use the record sheets as a simple tick list. It is more useful to indicate the frequency with which a child demonstrates a particular skill using words such as 'rarely', 'occasionally' and 'frequently'. It may be helpful to include an additional indicator of whether a skill has been fully mastered, such as 'with adult's support and encouragement' or 'independently'.

While bearing in mind that children develop at different rates, any marked difficulties in a given skills area should also be noted on the record sheets. A child with poor fine motor skills may, for example, be reluctant to write. For this child, a comment such as 'underlying motor skills not secure' would be a helpful indication of why that child performs less well in the area of writing skills.

Likewise, a child with a stammer may be reluctant to initiate conversation, and it would be sensible to indicate the possible reason for that child's poorer performance in certain skills.

© DIGITAL VISION

Letters and sounds

The most useful time to complete the letter/sound checklist (see example below) is towards the end of the Foundation Stage. To carry out the assessment, use the model to make an A4 record sheet to record the children's progress. Then make a cue card with letters set out in the same arrangement as on the record sheet. The letters should be clearly written in large, bold, lower-case print.

Present the card to the child with an appropriate introduction, saying that you would like them to show you what they can do. You can then explain that you would like the child to tell you the name of each of the letters in turn, indicating that they should work across the rows. Explain that the names of the letters are the names that we hear when we say the alphabet. Use the sheet to record correct answers with a slash in one direction, and incorrect answers by writing the letter named by the child. Note any long hesitations by writing an 'h' (hesitation) or any letters not named at all by an 'r' (refusal). If a sound is given write 's' (sound).

When the child has completed the card, invite them to go through it again, this time giving the letter sounds. Record answers as above, this time using an 'n' to indicate that the letter name was given instead of the sound. Note also if the child includes strong 'uh' sounds with the consonants.

Finally, remove the card and provide the child with a piece of lined paper. Explain that you would like them to write down letters as you name them. Work through the letters in the order given on the card, watching the child carefully. Record correctly formed letters with a slash, reversals with 'rev' and other errors with a brief comment such as 'started at top of letter'. Attach the child's writing sample to the record sheet noting on the sample any further comments about the child's writing posture and pen hold (see page 14).

Other assessment material

The Association for All Speech Impaired Children (AFASIC) produces extremely useful checklists for assessing language skills. The list for four- to five-year-olds would form a very helpful addition to the assessment procedures described above, producing more detailed information on a child's skills in the areas of language structure, language content and ability to communicate. This is a milestone checklist, meaning that the items included on the list indicate normal development, and it can be used to establish whether a child's speech and language skills are developing as might be expected. The check can be easily administered and scored by any practitioner who has regular contact with and is observing a child over a period of time.

The AFASIC language checklists can be obtained from LDA, Duke Street, Wisbech, Cambridgeshire PE13 2AE.

	i	t	p	n	s
name					
sound					
formation					

	k	a	c	h	d	b
name						
sound						
formation						

	e	o	f	l	y	g
name						
sound						
formation						

	q	r	m	u	j	w
name						
sound						
formation						

	z	x	v
name			
sound			
formation			

Early activities in this chapter provide the children with practice in communication skills such as vocabulary development. Later activities will encourage the children to engage in more sustained communication, such as storytelling.

Pass the mask

What to do
■ Ask the children to sit in a circle, and join them, taking your place among the children.
■ Explain that you are going to pass a message around the circle. Say that you will start and you will pass it to the person next to you, and that each person must pass the message on, until it gets back to you.
■ Next, explain that the message is not in words, but that you are going to tell the child sitting next to you how you are feeling by the look on your face. You are going to make your face into a 'message mask'.
■ Make a really happy face and ask for the 'mask' to be passed on around the group.
■ When the mask has passed right around the circle, ask one of the children to start with a new mask.
■ At the end of each round, ask the children what the mask told them about the sender's feelings.
■ With younger children, make it clear at the beginning of each round what feeling is being expressed. Say, 'This is a happy face' or invite the children to tell you what kind of face it is.
■ With older children, send two different mask messages at once, in opposite directions, around the circle.

More ideas
■ Play 'Change the mask' by shouting 'Change!' as the mask passes around. The person with the mask at that time must change it to a different one.
■ Try 'Touch telegraph' by sending a selected number of hand squeezes, winks, pats on the back or nudges, instead of facial expressions, around the group.

Other curriculum areas
| PD | Create 'Follow-my-leader' dances. |
| PSED | Read the book *Making Faces* by Nick Butterworth (Walker Books) and encourage |

the children to talk about what we can tell about a person's feelings from their face.

| CD | Invite the children to paint happy, sad and angry faces on sheets of A4 paper. |

Goals for the Foundation Stage

Stepping Stone
Use words and/or gestures, including body language such as eye contact and facial expression, to communicate.

Early Learning Goal
Interact with others, negotiating plans and activities and taking turns in conversation.

Group size
Up to 15 children.

What you need
A large space.

Home links
Ask parents and carers to play a 'Making faces' game with their children in front of a mirror, seeing who can make the happiest, saddest or angriest face.

Guess what I want

Early Learning Goal
Interact with others, negotiating plans and activities and taking turns in conversation.

Group size
Any size.

What you need
A packet of crisps; bar of chocolate; tin of baked beans; orange; hard-boiled egg in an egg-cup; banana; box of cereal; table.

Home links
Ask parents and carers to make sure that children have opportunities in their play to act out things that they have seen.

What to do
■ Show each of the food items to the children, then place all the items on a table.
■ Explain that each child in turn is going to tell the rest of the group what they would like to eat, but that no one is going to use any words. Say that, instead of words, they are going to act out how they would eat their chosen food. Then the rest of the group will try to guess what the food was.
■ Using the orange as an example, talk to the children about how you would need to peel it first, and then to separate out a segment. Demonstrate how you would mime this.
■ Choose a child and begin the game by inviting them to select a food item and to show how they would eat it. Encourage the other children to take turns to guess what the food is.
■ Once the group has guessed the food item, invite another child to choose a different food item and continue playing.
■ Help younger children by discussing, before they begin, what sort of actions they could use.
■ Ask older children to think of a food that is not on the table and to mime eating that.

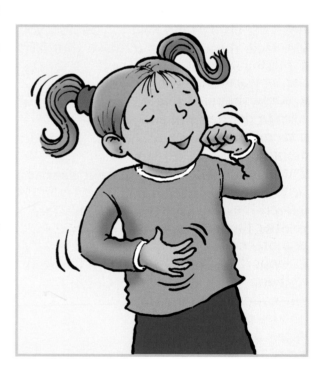

More ideas
■ Play 'What's the weather like?', with one child answering questions from the others by miming. Suggest questions such as, 'What does it feel like?', 'What would I wear?' and 'What could I do?'.
■ Provide puppets for the children to play with, encouraging them to think about movements and gestures that people make.

Other curriculum areas
KUW Look at books about people who use actions to help to send a message, such as the police directing traffic, airport runway controllers and train guards.

PSED Show the children how to cover their ears with their hands and to see how much they can understand of what is happening by just looking. Discuss what it is like not to be able to hear.

Going shopping

What to do

■ Read the book *Teddybears Go Shopping* to the children, then talk together about what went wrong with the shopping and why.

■ Explain to the children that they are going to play a shopping game. Ask them to decide who is going to play shopkeeper. If more than one child wants this role, suggest taking turns.

■ Tell the other children that they are each going to do some shopping. Invite them to decide what each of them will buy.

■ Suggest making one list, or perhaps more. Encourage discussion about which would be best. Provide paper and pencils so that the children can 'write' lists using marks, pictures or attempts at writing.

■ Send the children to do their shopping. When they return, talk about whether they remembered everything on their list, and if they helped each other.

■ Support younger children by drawing pictures to create shopping lists for them.

■ Encourage older children to shop for a particular event such as a birthday party.

More ideas

■ Draw up rules, together with the children, for taking turns to use the equipment.

■ Read stories that offer opportunities to talk about different points of view, for example, 'Goldilocks and the Three Bears' (Traditional).

Other curriculum areas

PD Let the children work in groups of three to form body pictures. For example, to make an elephant, one child holds their arms out straight in front to form the trunk, and the other two children, with arms on hips, form the ears. Ask the children to decide their roles.

MD Give the children numbered cards and invite them to work out together how to line up in order.

Stepping Stone
Initiate a conversation, negotiate positions, pay attention to and take account of others' views.

Early Learning Goal
Enjoy listening to and using spoken and written language, and readily turn to it in their play and learning.

Group size
Four to six children.

What you need
A copy of *Teddybears Go Shopping* by Susanna Gretz (Hippo) or a similar story about shopping that mentions items to be purchased; empty food packets or cartons for a role-play shop; table or playhouse that can serve as a shop; paper; pencils.

Preparation
Set up the role-play shop and put out all of the shopping items ready on the table.

Home links
Ask parents and carers to encourage their children to co-operate in tasks such as laying the table and to discuss with them who will carry out the various jobs.

Where did it go?

What to do
■ Explain to the children that they are going to experiment with different things and see what happens when they have water added to them.

■ Ask the children to measure a tablespoonful of sugar into one cup, and a tablespoonful of sand, coffee and marbles into each of the others. Make sure that they use level spoonfuls.

■ Now ask the children to measure a tablespoonful of warm water into each cup and to stir the contents of each cup together thoroughly but carefully.

■ Tell the children to look at the mixtures. Ask if they can still see the water in each cup and if they can still see the sugar, coffee and so on.

■ Encourage the children to talk about what they think has happened to the water and to the dry ingredients. Suggest that they feel the contents of the cups to see what this might tell them.

■ Help younger children to measure the ingredients. Suggest what might have happened in each cup, asking what they think.

■ Explain to older children that we have special words to describe what is happening in some of the cups, and introduce words such as 'dissolve' and 'absorb'.

More ideas
■ Experiment with different substances, for example, water, paint, sand and jam, to see which are soaked up quickly when a corner of paper towel is dipped into them.

■ Go out in the rain and watch it falling on different surfaces. Talk with the children about where the rain goes.

Other curriculum areas
CD Paint sheets of paper with water, then ask the children to paint arcs of colour on to the wet paper. Encourage them to talk about what is happening as the colours mix.

KUW Go on a plant-spotting walk with the children, to look for plants growing in unusual places, such as gutters and walls. Encourage the children to talk about how the plants might have got there.

What should Bear wear?

What to do

■ Introduce the children to your teddy bear. Give each child a copy of the photocopiable sheet and explain that there are some pictures of the teddy bear's clothes on it.

■ Tell the children that you are going to talk to them about some of the things that Bear does. For example, invite them to think about what Bear would wear to walk in the rain. Tell them to look at the sheet and to colour what he would wear in the rain yellow.

■ When they have finished colouring, ask them what they coloured and why they chose that article of clothing.

■ Work through all the clothing on the sheet in this way, asking what Bear should wear on the beach, on a cold day and to go to bed, assigning each item a separate colour according to your original plan.

■ With younger children, discuss which item they have chosen before they begin to colour.

■ Encourage older children to draw and colour further clothes for other occasions.

More ideas

■ Using a box of dressing-up clothes, give instructions such as 'Find something green to wear' or 'Find something to wear to a party'.

■ Give the children instructions for building a tower with a sequence of coloured bricks, and check at the end to see if everyone's tower looks the same.

Other curriculum areas

PD Play 'Simon Says' with the children to practise moving in a range of ways.

MD Give the children instructions for drawing things such as a house, shape by shape, for example, 'Draw a big square, now draw a triangle on top of the square, then two small squares in the big square' and so on.

PSED Hide an object in the room and give each child in turn one instruction to take them nearer to the object. Give the final instruction to all the children, so that they can find the object together.

Stepping Stone
Respond to simple instructions.

Early Learning Goal
Sustain attentive listening, responding to what they have heard by relevant comments, questions or actions.

Group size
Four to six children.

What you need
A copy of the photocopiable sheet 'Let's dress Bear' on page 83 for each child, and one for yourself; colouring crayons or felt-tipped pens; teddy bear.

Preparation
Decide which colour you want each item of clothing to be coloured and colour in your copy of the photocopiable sheet accordingly.

Home links
Ask carers to involve their children in simple household tasks that involve them following instructions, such as helping with baking.

The Three Little Pigs

Stepping Stone
Listen to favourite nursery rhymes, stories and songs. Join in with repeated refrains, anticipating key events and important phrases.

Early Learning Goal
Listen with enjoyment, and respond to stories, songs and other music, rhymes and poems and make up their own stories, songs, rhymes and poems.

Group size
Any size.

What you need
A copy of 'The Three Little Pigs' (Traditional).

Home links
Encourage parents and carers to read to their children regularly and explain how to pause periodically in their reading to encourage them to supply the next part of the story.

What to do
■ Show the book to the children and ask if anyone knows the story. Tell the children that this is a story that they will be able to join in with, even if they have not heard it before.
■ Begin to read the story. When you reach the refrains such as 'I'll huff and I'll puff', read these twice. Before your repeat them say, 'Listen very carefully to what the wolf said, and try to remember it'.
■ When you reach the repeat, read the first few words and then pause, placing your hand to your ear, inviting the children to join in. Ask questions to prompt them, such as, 'What do you think the wolf said, then?'. Praise all their attempts to join in with the refrain.
■ Help younger children by reminding them what happened, or what was said earlier, and asking them to repeat it.

■ Encourage older children to pre-empt the refrains, joining in at the appropriate point in the story. Challenge them to tell their own versions of the story.

More ideas
■ Try to create your own cue phrases for activities, so that the children can join in with them, for example, 'It's time for a drink now, so we're all going to...'.
■ Play nursery rhyme tapes. Turn down the sound and invite the children to continue with the rhyme. See if they are at the right point when you turn the sound up again.

Other curriculum areas
MD Share some number rhymes and encourage the children to join in.
KUW Look at information books that show how houses are built in other lands. Ask the children to consider whether the wolf would find these houses easy to blow down.
CD Build model houses from card, paper, recyclable materials and clay, and use them as props to retell the story of the Three Little Pigs or creating new versions.

Texture squares

What to do
■ Put the materials in the middle of a table and give each child a piece of A4 card.
■ Tell the children that they are going to make a 'feely' picture using materials that all feel different.
■ Ask the children to feel some of the squares from the collection, and to choose a square that they like the feel of.
■ Invite each child to tell you what their chosen square feels like and why they chose it.

■ Show the children how to brush a small amount of glue on to their cards in the top left corner, and ask each child to stick their square on to their card.
■ Next, invite the children to find a square that they do not like the feel of and to glue this next to their first square.
■ Continue until the A4 cards are covered. In turn ask the children to find squares that are bumpy, soft, hard, smooth, rough and so on.
■ With younger children, explain the meaning of the words that you use. Ask them, for example, to find a smooth square that their finger can slide over easily.
■ Encourage older children to make their own selection of squares, explaining to you why they have chosen each one and describing what it feels like.

More ideas
■ Read *Old Hat, New Hat* by Stan Berenstain (Collins) and ask the children to describe the clothes they themselves are wearing.
■ Hold a food-tasting session and talk about how different foods feel in the mouth and taste. Check for any food allergies or dietary requirements.

Other curriculum areas
MD Carry out a survey to see how many children have hair that is curly, straight, short and so on. Use different-coloured DUPLO bricks for each category and ask the children to each add a brick to make towers for each type of hair.

KUW Investigate different animal patterns with the children and make a display of their pattern drawings, labelled with pattern words.

Stepping Stone
Build up vocabulary that reflects the breadth of their experiences.

Early Learning Goal
Extend their vocabulary, exploring the meanings and sounds of new words.

Group size
Four children.

What you need
A collection of squares of different-textured materials, such as fabric, paper, card and bubble wrap; sheet of A4 card for each child; glue; glue brushes; table.

Preparation
Cut the collected materials into 5cm squares.

Home links
Suggest that parents and carers take every opportunity to talk to their children about what they see around them, using a range of different describing words.

Animal fun

Early Learning Goal
Extend their vocabulary, exploring the meanings and sounds of new words.

Group size
Four children.

What you need
A copy of the book *Dear Zoo* by Rod Campbell (Puffin Books) or any lift-the-flap book that includes a sequence of hidden animals; drawings or pictures of each of the animals in the book; thin card; glue; scissors.

Preparation
Make a set of picture cards to show the animals that appear in the book, by gluing the drawings or pictures on to squares of card.

What to do

■ Explain to the children that you are going to read a story and then play a game to find out what they can remember.
■ Read the book *Dear Zoo*, pausing before you lift each flap to allow the children to guess which animal has been sent.
■ Next, spread the picture cards out on the table and ask the children to try to remember which animal the zoo sent first. Remind them that it was an animal that was too big.

■ Work through the animals in this way, using words such as 'next', 'after' and 'last' in your questions. As the children select the animals, move the cards into the correct sequence.
■ Provide additional clues for younger children, mentioning a trunk, a hump and so on.
■ Use more complex clues for older children, asking them what the zoo sent after the giraffe and before the camel. Let them sequence the cards independently.

More ideas

■ Hide objects in a bowl of very soapy water. Let the children feel around and name what they pick up, saying things such as, 'I think it's a sponge, because it's soft and squidgy'.
■ Ask the children to sort shells into groups by colour, shape, size and attractiveness, and to explain how they decided which shells belonged to which group.

Home links

Ask parents and carers to talk frequently with their children about their daily routine, reminding them of the order in which certain things will happen. Encourage them to link activities with specific days of the week and to talk about which day follows another.

Other curriculum areas

PD Line up six children, then give instructions to shuffle the line, asking one child to move and stand after X and in front of Y.

KUW Send the children to explore the room, then to come back and name as many things as they can that are made of wood, plastic and so on.

A special time

What to do

■ Invite the children to sit in a group with a clear view of you.

■ Show your photograph and say that it was taken at a time that was special for you. Model questions by asking, 'Would you like to know why this day was special?' or 'What do you think I felt like?'.

■ Talk about where you were, what you wore, how you felt, and who was there with you. Ask the children if they have anything that they would like to ask you about your special time.

■ Remind the children that you asked them to bring in a photograph of a special time and tell them that they are now going to talk to everyone about their special day.

■ Choose a child to begin and ask them to show everyone their photo and to talk about their special time.

■ Encourage questions from the other children when the child has finished speaking.

■ With younger children, use encouraging prompts to help maintain the flow of what they are saying. Suggest, for example, that they might like to tell everyone who else was with them.

■ Older children can be encouraged to talk about their special time without needing a model from you.

Other curriculum areas

PSED Provide opportunities for the children to talk about celebrations in their own cultures, encouraging interest in cultural and religious differences.

CD Let the children take turns to show their paintings and models to the other children and to talk about how they made them or what they represent.

More ideas

■ Have a 'pet day' and invite the children to bring in photos of their pets, or a picture of an animal that they would like for a pet, to talk about.

■ Using a teddy as a focus, talk about what he might do at night, when you are asleep. Ask the children to talk about what their favourite cuddly toys might do while they are sleeping.

How and why?

Stepping Stone
Consistently develop a simple story, explanation or line of questioning.

Early Learning Goal
Speak clearly and audibly with confidence and control and show awareness of the listener.

Group size
Any size.

What you need
Recyclable materials for construction and modelling; scissors; glue; commercially produced construction kits.

Preparation
Set out some tables with the recyclable materials for construction. Provide an area where the commercially produced construction kits can be used.

Home links
Encourage parents and carers to allow their children to contribute to conversations at home, and to provide them with the chance to talk about their day.

What to do

■ Tell the children that they are going to make a building. Say that it can be real or imaginary, and make some suggestions for real buildings such as fire stations, hospitals, garages and space stations. Invite the children to contribute further suggestions. Encourage them to talk about imaginary buildings, too.

■ Explain that they can choose to construct their buildings from the recyclable materials or from the kits. Show them some of the recyclable materials and ask them how they think the items could be used.

■ Encourage some of the children to tell you what they have decided to make, then let them begin work.

■ As the children work, ask questions about what they are using and why they have chosen particular materials.

■ When the models are complete, invite the children to describe what they have built to everyone else. Encourage them to explain how they went about the task and why they chose to use certain materials.

■ Help younger children to decide what to build before they begin work, and suggest materials that might be appropriate.

■ Challenge older children to create a building of a minimum height, providing a piece of string as a measure.

More ideas

■ Go on a 'wondering walk', modelling questions about things that you see, for example, 'I wonder why the leaves on the trees are moving'. Encourage the children's explanations, whether these are real or imaginary.

■ Play 'Can you guess what I'm thinking of?', giving a clue such as 'It's an animal'. Encourage the children to ask you questions that might help them to guess which animal you have in mind.

Other curriculum areas

PSED Put the children in pairs and ask them to find out their partner's favourite food, colour and animal, by asking questions.

PD Ask the children to each move around the room like an animal. Select children to demonstrate their movements and to explain why they chose that animal.

The activities in this chapter will help the children to develop their thinking skills. They will be encouraged to talk through actions, make predictions and test their validity, discuss imaginary situations and retell experiences.

Balancing trick

What to do
■ Explain to the children that they are going to help you solve a problem. Give each child a marble and invite them to place it on the board.
■ When the marbles roll off, ask the children to help you to make the board even, so that the marbles will stay still on it. Show them the alternative supports and ask if they think that they could use these to help to solve the problem.

■ Encourage the children to look at the slope of the board and to think about what they need to do to make it more even. Suggest that they experiment with the remaining supports and ask them to test the slope with the marbles each time that they make an adjustment.
■ Be more explicit with younger children, showing them how to use some of the other supports to raise the lower end of the slope.
■ With older children, do not provide further supports, but ask them to suggest things that could be used to even the slope of the board.

More ideas
■ Provide a stable slope and marbles and invite the children to make a maze from a variety of objects for the marbles to roll through.
■ Challenge the children to create a maze of noisy objects on the slope, which the marbles can hit to make a noise as they pass along.

Other curriculum areas
PD ■ Use chalk to draw an imaginary river on the ground and ask the children to find the best way of placing cardboard 'stepping-stones' to make it easy to cross the river.

KUW ■ Provide containers with wider and narrower necks, for example, jugs, funnels and plastic tubing, and let the children talk about and experiment with the best way to fill each container.

Goals for the **Foundation Stage**

Stepping Stone
Talk activities through, reflecting on and modifying what they are doing.

Early Learning Goal
Use language to imagine and re-create roles and experiences.
■
Group size
Four children.
■
What you need
A board approximately 50 cm square; supports of differing heights and thicknesses, such as books, blocks and tins; four marbles.
■
Preparation
Place the board on supports of uneven heights so that it forms a wobbly slope. Have other supports close by.

Home links
Suggest that parents and carers give their children experience of weighing, pouring and measuring activities. Explain that children learn by seeing the results of their actions, then adjusting what they do next time. Emphasise that this is important even if they make a mess.

Lift off!

Stepping Stone
Talk activities through, reflecting on and modifying what they are doing.

Early Learning Goal
Use language to imagine and re-create roles and experiences.

Group size
Three or four children.

What you need
Clean packaging, including cardboard boxes, cereal boxes, plastic pots and cardboard rolls; glue; scissors; split-pin fasteners; bendy straws; long, thick pipe-cleaners; sticky tape; information books such as *The Usborne First Encyclopedia of Space* (Usborne).

Home links
Explain to parents and carers that talking through a simple activity helps children to develop good thinking skills.

What to do
■ Explain to the children that they are each going to make a control centre for a spaceship. Look at information books together to get some ideas of what a space station might look like.
■ Encourage the children to talk about how they want their models to look and ask them which materials they will use.
■ Give each child a cardboard box to use as a base unit. Invite the children to start their models, and work alongside them.
■ Talk about what you might use for a control centre. Suggest that plastic pots joined together by a pipe-cleaner could make good headphones. 'Wonder' out loud whether a bendy straw taped to one of the headphones might make a good microphone. Help the children to cut out cardboard dials and to fit them to the cardboard boxes with split-pin fasteners.
■ Use some of the children's ideas on your model and ask whether they would like to try some of your ideas.
■ If the children are having problems developing their own ideas, suggest how they can achieve their goal, or that they may need to change their ideas a little.
■ Help younger children with fine motor tasks such as cutting and taping.
■ Challenge older children to think of ways in which they could use particular materials.

More ideas
■ Let the children make clothes for toys, using tissues, paper and fabric scraps tied on with wool or ribbons.
■ Ask the children to build a strong bridge across a bowl of water for a toy car to cross. Encourage them to test paper, card and a ruler to find the best material.

Other curriculum areas
CD Provide pulses and a collection of identical containers. Talk about how to fill the containers to produce shakers that make different sounds.

KUW Put tissue-paper fish on the floor and ask the children to work out how to use newspapers to make the fish move. They will discover that they need to flap the paper close to the fish but without the paper touching it.

Moon landing

What to do
■ Read *The Bears Who Stayed Indoors* (or any story about space travel) to the children. Explain that they are going to play a game about travelling to the moon.
■ Put on aprons. Show the children the paper and paint and tell them that first they must make a moon.
■ Next, suggest that they use the play dough to make some 'moon biscuits' to take with them on their journey.

■ Show them the cardboard boxes and tell them that these are going to be turned into space helmets. Fold the flaps of one of the boxes up inside and use a craft knife to cut a square in the side to create a visor.
■ Let the children paint the moon and make the 'biscuits' while you cut the remaining visors in the other boxes.
■ Pin up the picture of the moon and let the children pretend play going to the moon. If you have made the space control centre from the activity 'Lift off!', let the children use this, too.
■ With younger children, make the props for the game in advance and present them ready for play.
■ Encourage older children to think of other things that they could use in the game.

More ideas
■ Read *The Tiger Who Came to Tea* by Judith Kerr (Picture Lions) as the stimulus for creating a meal for a tiger from play items.
■ Make drums from upturned pans, boxes and cans, and drumsticks from wooden spoons.

Other curriculum areas
MD Invite the children to use DUPLO bricks to represent sweets for counting games.
KUW Cut 'dinosaur feet' from stiff cardboard. Make two holes and thread elastic through to fit over the children's feet, so that they can make 'dinosaur footprints' in soft sand.

Stepping Stone
Use talk to give new meanings to objects and actions, treating them as symbols for other things.

Early Learning Goal
Use language to imagine and re-create roles and experiences.
■

Group size
Five children.
■

What you need
A copy of *The Bears Who Stayed Indoors* by Susanna Gretz (A & C Black) or any story about space travel; aprons; black sugar paper; yellow paint; paintbrushes; yellow play dough; pastry roller and cutter; cardboard boxes; craft knife; space control centre from the activity 'Lift off!' on page 30 (optional).
■

Preparation
Make the props for the game ready for younger children.

Home links
Help parents and carers with ideas for imaginative play using simple objects: a bed can serve as a boat, with a large spatula as an oar; an armchair can be turned into a car, with a saucepan lid for a steering wheel, and so on.

Whatever is it?

Stepping Stone
Begin to use talk to pretend imaginary situations.

Early Learning Goal
Use language to imagine and re-create roles and experiences.
■

Group size
Three children.
■

What you need
A copy of *The Quangle Wangle's Hat* by Edward Lear (Little Mammoth); paper; pencils; colouring crayons.

What to do
■ Read *The Quangle Wangle's Hat* to the children, drawing their attention to the imaginary creatures in the poem. Tell them that they are going to help each other to make up their own strange creatures. Talk about the things in the poem that make the creatures strange, such as a corkscrew leg.

■ Give each child a piece of paper and ask them to draw and colour the head of an imaginary creature.

■ When they have finished, tell them to pass the paper to the next child and to add a body to the picture that they now have.

■ Invite the children to pass the paper on again, and this time to add legs to the pictures.

■ Let each child give a name to the creature that they have completed. Ask questions about what the creatures like to eat, where they live, and so on. Encourage the children to talk about what they would do if they met one of these creatures.

■ Let younger children draw the whole of their fantasy creature, rather than adding to the drawings of other children.

■ Ask older children to fold down the paper to hide what they have drawn before they pass it on.

More ideas
■ Provide stimulating play environments. For example, to create a jungle, tape crêpe-paper streamers around a table edge, use kitchen-roll tubes, sticky tape and string to make binoculars, and hide toy animals among cushion 'rocks'.

■ Create a building site with toy vehicles and piles of dry lentils, pasta and so on as building materials. Ask the children to talk through what is happening as they play.

Other curriculum areas
CD Play *Carnival of the Animals* by Saint Saëns and invite the children to close their eyes and then tell you how they imagined the animals as they heard the music.

PSED Provide the children with props for hospital role-play, such as bandages marked with red felt-tipped pen. Encourage them to act out roles as patients and carers.

Home links
Show parents and carers how their children can use readily available items to create imaginary situations. For example, a toy animal, a cardboard box and a paper plate can be used to act out what it would be like to look after a pet.

What happened next?

What to do

■ Read *On the Way Home* to the children. Pause at the end of each of Claire's explanations about how she got her bad knee, to ask the children if they think that this really happened.

■ At the end of the story, explain that Claire was trying to be very brave about her bad knee. Ask the children if they have ever hurt themselves.

■ Let the children tell their stories of when they hurt themselves.

■ Remind the children that Claire hurt herself at the park. Ask them if they have ever been to the park, and what they did there. Encourage the children to talk about their experiences.

■ Explain to the children that you would now like them to make up some stories like Claire did. Ask if anyone has ever met a wolf, or another scary character from the story. Encourage the children in their storytelling by asking them questions about where events happened and how they felt.

■ Finish by asking if anyone has really had something scary happen to them.

■ With younger children, focus only on real events that have happened to them.

■ Invite older children to make up some more stories that Claire might have told.

More ideas

■ Use traditional rhymes as an introduction to the children talking about their own experiences. For example, 'Mary Had a Little Lamb' could introduce the subject of pets.

■ Visit a local pond, then act out 'Five Little Speckled Frogs' (Traditional). Encourage the children to change the rhyme to include creatures that they saw at the pond.

Other curriculum areas

MD Provide a simple line drawing of a birthday cake and ask the children to draw on the correct number of candles for their age, and to write the number on the cake. Use this as a stimulus to talk about how they celebrated their birthday.

CD After a walk on a windy day, let the children make pictures by blowing small pools of thin paint over paper. As they work, encourage them to talk about the things that they saw being blown about by the wind.

Stepping Stone
Begin to use talk instead of action to reflect on past experience, linking significant events from own experience and from stories.

Early Learning Goal
Use language to imagine and re-create roles and experiences.
■
Group size
Any size.
■
What you need
A copy of *On the Way Home* by Jill Murphy (Macmillan).

Home links
Let the children borrow books that provide opportunities for them to talk about their own similar experiences, or make recommendations of suitable books to parents and carers.

One too many

What to do
■ Read *Mr Gumpy's Outing* to the children. As each animal is added to the boat, ask the children what they think will happen if that animal does not behave as Mr Gumpy wants it to.

■ Show the boat to the children and explain that they are going to test how many DUPLO figures can fit into it, without it sinking. Ask each of the children to make a guess at how many figures the boat will safely carry.

■ Place the boat on the water and invite each child in turn to place a figure in the boat. Make sure that they do this carefully, so that they do not upturn or sink the boat by accident. Continue adding figures until the boat sinks. Count how many figures were in the boat before the last one was added. Check the total against the children's original guesses.

■ As each figure is added, ask younger children whether they think that this might be the last one before the boat sinks.

■ Invite older children to estimate how many figures there are, before they count them.

More ideas
■ Upturn a shoebox and cut doors in one of its narrow ends. Present the children with toy cars and ask them to guess how many will fit into the shoebox garage. Let them check if their estimates are correct.

■ Start to read a story that is unfamiliar to the children. Encourage them to talk about what they think will happen next.

Other curriculum areas
PSED Show the children pictures of celebrations in other cultures and invite them to discuss what is happening in them.

CD Demonstrate how to mix paint colours and encourage the children to predict the colour that they will make if they mix two or more particular colours, or if they add white to their mix.

Watch that car!

What to do

■ Explain to the children that they are going to do some experiments with toy cars and invite each child to choose a car.

■ Ask the children which car they think will reach the bottom of the slope first, if they let both cars run down together. Encourage them to test their guess, making sure that the cars are released at the same time.

■ Discuss why they think that the winning car was first. Ask what might happen if they make the slope steeper. Help them to prop the slope higher and experiment again.

■ Try different angles of slope, then cover the board with a tea towel and experiment again. Try wetting the tea towel. Always ask the children what they think will happen first, and discuss why they think a particular car won, after each trial.

■ Help younger children by talking about the different weight or shape of cars as possible reasons why one car might be faster than another.

■ Encourage older children to play a group of cars off against one another, predicting which will be the overall winner.

More ideas

■ Grow cress in empty eggshells with faces drawn on them. Place them in different places and invite the children to say which will grow the 'best hair'.

■ Fill cocoa tins with differing weights of marbles or stones. Let the children predict which 'road roller' will make the flattest road across the sand-pit.

Other curriculum areas

KUW Place ice cubes in different places around the room and invite the children to guess which will melt first. Talk about the results.

PD Sit a soft toy on the floor and ask the children if it will look the same from everywhere in the room. Give instructions such as 'Take three steps, bend over and look at it through your legs'. Discuss what they can see.

Pass the story

Early Learning Goal
Use talk to organise, sequence and clarify thinking, ideas, feelings and events.

Group size
Four to six children.

What you need
A selection of postcards with pictures suitable as a stimulus for storytelling (places, people or events); any story-book.

Home links
Encourage parents and carers to instigate imaginative play such as picnics 'at the beach' using the sand-pit, or a trip on a 'magic carpet' using a rug or blanket on the living-room floor.

What to do
■ Read the story-book to the children.
■ Explain to the children that they are going to make up their own story and show them one of the postcards.
■ Tell the children that you are going to start a story about the picture on the card. Say that you want them to listen very carefully. Explain that you will then give the card to one of them, and that this child should add another bit to the story, then pass the card on. Each person should add something to the story.

■ As each child makes a contribution, try to repeat the whole story so far, to aid their understanding of the continuing story line. As the children's ideas peter out, use your turn to bring the story to a conclusion.
■ Help younger children by asking them questions, so that their answers form their contribution to the story.
■ Write down the stories created by older children and keep them alongside the relevant postcard. See if the children can retell them at a later date.

Other curriculum areas
PD Tell the story of 'The Three Billy Goats Gruff' (Traditional). Provide a low plank or PE bench as a bridge and ask the children to tell and show you different ways to cross the bridge to escape the troll.
MD Set up a 'baby clinic' where the children can weigh and measure the dolls and teddies.
CD Make paper-bag puppets by drawing faces on plain paper bags and placing small elastic bands on the corners to create ears (see illustration). Make up a play using these.

More ideas
■ Pretend that the climbing frame is a mountain, and ask the children to climb it and describe all the things that they can see from the top.
■ Cover a table with a cloth to form a dark 'cave'. Tape silver-paper 'stalactites' to the underneath of the table and let the children explore the cave with a torch, encouraging them to describe their feelings and what they can and cannot see.

What goes where?

What to do
■ Show the children the house outline and discuss what the various rooms are called.
■ Explain to the children that you have some pictures of things that you would find in a house. Tell them that you need some help to sort out in which rooms the things belong.
■ Choose one of the pictures and ask the children in which of the rooms this item would be found. Ask them to put the picture in the correct room on the house.
■ Invite the children to sort the remaining pictures into the correct rooms.
■ Help younger children by focusing on one room at a time and working through all the pictures to find the items that belong in this room.
■ Allow older children to sort the pictures into the correct rooms without discussing the names of the rooms first, and include some pictures of items that might be found in more than one room. Ask the children to explain why they have placed items in particular rooms.

More ideas
■ Sort pictures of dogs in as many different ways as possible, using groups such as 'long tails', 'big ears' and 'pointed noses'.
■ Draw a set of pictures of a flower at different stages of growth and ask the children to put the pictures in order.

Other curriculum areas
KUW Give each of seven children an item of clothing to wear, each in a different colour of the rainbow. Show the children a picture of a rainbow and invite them to sort themselves into the correct colour order.
PD Sing action songs that contain repeated sequences of movements, such as 'The Hokey Cokey' (Traditional).
MD Sort the children's teddy bears into different hoops according to whether they are large, medium or small in size.

Stepping Stone
Begin to make patterns in their experience through linking cause and effect, sequencing, ordering and grouping.

Early Learning Goal
Use talk to organise, sequence and clarify thinking, ideas, feelings and events.
■
Group size
Four children.
■
What you need
Pictures of everyday household items, cut from magazines or catalogues; sheet of A2 card; thin card; glue.
■
Preparation
Glue the pictures on to pieces of thin card. Draw a simple house outline (see illustration) on to the A2 card.

Home links
Encourage parents and carers to involve their children in grouping activities such as sorting different-coloured clothes for washing, and putting away toys in specific storage places.

In the holidays

Early Learning Goal
Use talk to organise, sequence and clarify thinking, ideas, feelings and events.

Group size
Any size.

What you need
Toy boat, car, plane and train; small suitcase; holiday items such as a swimsuit, bucket and spade, sun-glasses and camera; postcards of different types of destinations, such as a beach, the countryside and a city; table.

Home links
Ask parents and carers to look back through family photographs with their children, talking about and sharing past experiences.

What to do

■ Invite the children to sit comfortably on the floor. Explain that you are going to tell them about your holiday, and then ask some of them to talk about their holiday. Place all the items on the table.

■ Begin by telling the children where you went and showing them an appropriate postcard. Hold up the relevant toy (boat, car, plane or train) as you say which method of transport you used. Hold up the suitcase as you talk about the sort of things that you took with you. Tell the children what the weather was like, putting on the sun-glasses, for example, to emphasise hot weather. Say what you did, showing items such as a bucket and spade to talk about the beach.

■ Invite one of the children to come and talk about a holiday that they have enjoyed. Ask them to pick up and show any items that will help them to tell the story of their holiday.

■ Help younger children by asking questions. Point to each toy vehicle in turn, asking if they travelled by car, train, boat or plane.

■ Ask older children to choose three things only from the table to help them tell their holiday story.

More ideas

■ Go on a 'memory walk' and ask the children to collect one thing, such as a leaf, to remind them of the walk. Afterwards, encourage the children to talk about why they chose their collected item, and how it helps to remind them of the walk.

■ Select pictures to act as a focus for 'Has anyone here ever...?' sessions. Choose pictures of places that the children may have visited, such as farms, parks and so on.

Other curriculum areas

PSED Ask the children to bring in objects associated with special celebration times, such as Christmas, Divali or Eid, and to talk about their experiences.

KUW After a trip with the children, make a group 'guidebook' with photographs and the children's drawings. Use it to stimulate memories of the visit later.

In this chapter there are activities that are designed to help the children to distinguish sounds within words and to link sounds to appropriate letters. Ideas include focusing on the beats within words, and showing that matching sound patterns are written with matching letter patterns.

Drum beat

What to do

■ Explain to the children that you are going to read a book that is a bit like a song, and that you want them to say the words back to you and to clap the beats in the words as they say them.

■ Read the first page, clapping the beats as you read. Ask the children to repeat the words and the clapping.

■ Then read one page at a time (the text on each page is very short), modelling the clapping, and invite the children to repeat both the words and the clapping.

■ Read the pages more slowly for younger children and limit the clapping to the 'sound effects' sections of the text. Experiment to see if some children find it easier to beat on a table with one hand, rather than to clap.

■ With older children, model the clapping for the first page. Then say the words only for the following pages, allowing the children to add the clapping for themselves. Try speeding up the reading.

More ideas

■ Working round the group, clap the beats in each child's name.

■ When you give general instructions to the whole group, clap out the beats as you speak. Ask the children to repeat the instruction back to you, clapping as they do so.

Other curriculum areas

CD Use different songs to practise clapping beats. For variety, stamp the beats, or provide drums and tambourines. Improvise instruments with tins and spoons.

PD Make a tally chart of how many children in the group have names with one beat, two beats and so on.

MD Draw boxes on the floor and encourage the children to hop or jump from one box to another as they say the beats of words that you call out.

Stepping Stone
Enjoy rhyming and rhythmic activities.

Early Learning Goal
Hear and say initial and final sounds in words, and short vowel sounds within words.

■

Group size
Any size.

■

What you need
A copy of *Hand, Hand, Fingers, Thumb* by Al Perkins (Collins).

■

Preparation
Read through the book *Hand, Hand, Fingers, Thumb* so that you can read it aloud with a strong sense of rhythm.

Home links
Encourage parents and carers to read nursery rhymes and poems to their children, helping them to clap the rhythm as they read.

The same or different?

Early Learning Goal
Hear and say initial and final sounds in words, and short vowel sounds within words.

Group size
Four to six children.

What you need
A copy of the photocopiable sheet 'The same sound?' on page 84 for each child; colouring crayons or felt-tipped pens.

What to do
■ Give each child a copy of the photocopiable sheet.
■ Explain that they are going to be listening carefully for the sounds at the beginning of words.
■ Ask them to look at the first pair of pictures (sun and sand-castle) and to say the name of the first picture. Tell them to listen very carefully to the first sound in the word.
■ Now invite them to say the name of the second picture, again listening very carefully for the first sound in the word.
■ Tell them to colour both pictures in the same colour if they think that both of the words start with the same sound. If they think that the two words start with a different sound, they should colour the pictures with different colours.
■ Use the same instructions for each pair of pictures.
■ Help younger children to separate out and identify the first sound of each word, after they have said it, before they colour the pictures.
■ Encourage older children to draw pictures of two things that begin with the same sound, and then two that begin with different sounds.

More ideas
■ Ask the children to find two things in the room that begin with the same sound.
■ Invite the children to say their names and to see if any of them begin with the same sound.

Home links
Encourage parents and carers to invite their children to look for things that start with the same sound as they unpack the shopping, for example, seeing how many things in the bag begin with the same sound as 'sausages'.

Other curriculum areas
KUW Look through animal books with the children to find out about animals whose names begin with the same sound.

MD Count out two groups of objects with numbers that begin with the same sound.

PD Give the children instructions for action rhymes, emphasising the first sounds in words, for example, 'We're going to wave our h-h-h-hands in the air'.

Communication, language and literacy

In the hat

What to do

■ Place the set of picture cards, face down, on the table. Give each child one of the containers and ask them to name it and to tell you the sound at the beginning of that word.

■ Explain to the children that you want them, in turn, to pick up a card from the pack. They must name the picture on that card and say the sound at the beginning of the word. If the picture starts with the same sound as their container, they can put the card into their container. If not, they must place the card back at the bottom of the pack. Explain that the first person to have three cards in their container is the winner.

■ Pick up the first card, identify the picture and the sound, and show the children which container it belongs to. Place it back in the pack. Begin the game after checking that the children remember the initial sounds of their containers.

■ With younger children, spread out all cards, face up, on the table. Choose one container at a time and work as a group to find all the correct pictures.

■ Give older children a container and ask them to make four new cards with appropriate pictures for their container.

More ideas

■ Provide other containers (a jug, sock, cup, glove, pan and so on) and cards for the different initial sounds.

■ Use containers with different end sounds and make appropriate sets of cards.

Other curriculum areas

PD Say a letter sound and invite the children to move like an animal beginning with that sound.

KUW Prepare for a visit by saying that the children may see something beginning with a particular sound. Ask them for suggestions, then try other sounds.

MD Encourage the children to collect ten items from around the room and to group them according to their initial sounds. Are there more items beginning with any one sound?

Stepping Stone
Hear and say the initial sound in words and know which letters represent some of the sounds.

Early Learning Goal
Hear and say initial and final sounds in words, and short vowel sounds within words.

Group size
Four children.

What you need
The photocopiable sheet 'Say the sounds' on page 85; four containers (bag, hat, tin and mug); thin card; glue; scissors; table.

Preparation
Copy the photocopiable sheet on to thin card. Cut around the individual pictures.

Home links
Ask parents and carers to play 'I spy' with their children, using letter *sounds* only.

Bag the sound

Stepping Stone
Hear and say the initial sound in words and know which letters represent some of the sounds.

Early Learning Goal
Hear and say initial and final sounds in words, and short vowel sounds within words.

Group size
Three children.

What you need
Three carrier bags; three sets of four objects beginning with the same sound, for example, pen, pencil, paper and paintbrush; three corresponding plastic or wooden letters; table.

Preparation
Place all the objects randomly on the table. Put the bags on it as well, with a letter on top of each one.

Home links
Encourage carers to play 'I spy' with their children using letter *names*.

What to do
■ Ask one child to hand you an object and to name it. Can they say which sound comes at the beginning of that word?

■ Invite each child to find another object beginning with the same sound, and challenge them to name the object and say the initial sound.

■ Explain that one of the letters on the bags 'writes' that sound. Ask which letter it is.

■ Place all four objects and the appropriate letter in the bag together.

■ Encourage the next child to choose another object from the table, and repeat the procedure, until all the corresponding objects and letters have been placed in bags.

■ Show younger children each letter before you begin the activity and tell them the sound that the letter 'writes'.

■ Invite older children to group together the objects that begin with the same sound and then to place them in the bag with the letter that 'writes' the sound. Close your eyes while they work and then check each bag in turn.

More ideas
■ Give each child a plastic or wooden letter. Ask them to hold up their letter and name it if you say a word that begins with their letter sound.

■ Place small objects in a bag and invite each child to take out an object and to find the correct letter, from a group of wooden letters on the table, to 'write' the first sound. Ask them to name the letter.

Other curriculum areas
PD Provide bold outlines of letter shapes and invite the children to colour them in a colour that has that letter sound at the beginning, for example, yellow for the letter 'y'.

CD Draw large letters in chalk on the ground and ask the children to move along each letter in a way that reflects the sound of the letter. For example, they could walk along 'w', run along 'r' and jump along 'j'.

Communication, language and literacy

Feel the letter

What to do

■ Show the pictures to the children and invite them to tell you what they can see. Ask them which sound comes at the beginning of all the words.

■ Explain that they are going to use Plasticine or play dough to make the letter that 'writes' this sound. Name the letter.

■ Use the Plasticine or play dough to make the letter, explaining how you are making it. Ask the children to copy what you do.

■ Show the children how to trace over the letter shape with their fingers. Check that they begin at the correct position and copy your movement exactly.

■ Give each child a pencil and a piece of card and encourage them to write the letter, copying you.

■ Ask the children to tell you the letter sound and its name again.

■ Send the children around the room to look for things that begin with the sound that they have written. Tell them to put their cards beside one thing that they find.

■ Provide ready-rolled Plasticine for younger children. Help them to form letters and guide their hands as they write.

■ Encourage older children to show you how to make the letter shape from Plasticine of play dough.

More ideas

■ Write letters on pieces of card, put a paper clip on each card and place them in a container. Make a fishing line with a magnet, and ask the children to 'fish' for a letter and think up things that begin with that letter sound.

■ Start a sound collection. Write a letter on a card and place it on a table. Ask the children to bring in items that begin with that letter sound.

Other curriculum areas

MD Make a bar chart of the initial letters of the children's names.

KUW Bake biscuits and help the children to use decorations laid out in letter shapes.

Stepping Stone
Hear and say the initial sound in words and know which letters represent some of the sounds.

Early Learning Goal
Link sounds to letters, naming and sounding the letters of the alphabet.
■

Group size
Four children.
■

What you need
Plasticine or play dough; pencils; thin card; pictures of objects beginning with the 'focus' sound.
■

Preparation
Cut four 10cm squares from the card. Check that there are objects around the room that begin with the sound of the focus letter.

Home links
Suggest that parents and carers make a letter/sound book with their children by writing a letter on each page and sticking pictures from magazines of things beginning with that letter sound.

Letter maze

What to do

■ Give a copy of the maze and a pencil to each child. Show the children the way into the maze and the way out of the maze.

■ Tell the children that they are going to find the way through the maze by following the letters of the alphabet. Explain that they must follow the letters in the right order to find their way through the maze correctly.

■ Encourage the children to say the alphabet out loud as they work as this will help them to remember the letter that they are looking for next.

■ Explain that they are not allowed to cross any lines in the maze to reach a letter, and they should try to stay in the middle of the pathways from one letter to the next.

■ Help younger children by placing an alphabet strip on the table in front of each of them. Give them a counter, which they can move along the strip to keep their place as they go through the maze.

■ Provide older children with alphabet strips that have one or two letters missing, and encourage them to try to find out what the missing letters are.

More ideas

■ Use dot-to-dot books to reinforce alphabet skills. White out the numbers and replace them with the letters of the alphabet. Add or delete dots to obtain the correct number.

■ Put plastic or wooden letters out on a table and ask the children to arrange them in alphabetical order, in the shape of a rainbow arc.

Other curriculum areas

PD Draw an alphabet snake on the ground, with a letter in each segment. Ask the children to make their way along the snake by throwing a beanbag onto a segment and hopping along to it, saying the alphabet as they go.

KUW Place a telephone directory in the home corner and show the children how the names are arranged.

Match the rhyme

What to do

■ Lay the plastic or wooden alphabet out in an arc on a table. Lay the cards out on one side of the table.

■ Place a cue picture card below the arc and invite the children to tell you what they can see.

■ Ask the children what the first sound in the word is and encourage them to look for the letter that 'writes' this sound. Help them to find the letters that spell the rest of the sounds in the word.

■ Explain that two other cards have pictures that rhyme with this card. Ask the children to find one each. Let them check their pictures by fitting them together with the cue picture.

■ As each picture is matched, encourage the child to change the initial letter of the first word to make the rhyming word for the new card.

■ Start again with a new cue card and repeat the activity.

■ Help younger children to hear that the ends of rhyming words sound the same and that only the beginning sound is different. Spell out the cue word for them and help them to change the initial letter to make the rhyming words.

■ Encourage older children to think up more words that rhyme with the cue word, and to build these by changing the first letter.

More ideas

■ Collect pairs of rhyming pictures and use them to make a Pelmanism game to play with the children.

■ Begin a nursery rhyme, but leave out a rhyming word. Ask the children to supply a different silly rhyming word, for example, 'Ring-o-Ring-o-Roses, A pocketful of noses'.

Other curriculum areas

PSED Teach the children rhymes for choosing people fairly for games.

MD Share some counting rhymes.

CD Use nursery rhymes to stimulate artwork. For example, read 'Little Miss Muffet' (Traditional), then encourage the children to glue wool on to card to make spiders' webs.

Stepping Stone
Continue a rhyming string.

Early Learning Goal
Link sounds to letters, naming and sounding the letters of the alphabet.

■

Group size
Pairs of children.

■

What you need
The photocopiable sheet 'Make new words' on page 87; thin card; glue; scissors; plastic or wooden alphabet letters.

■

Preparation
Copy the photocopiable sheet on to thin card. Cut around the individual pictures.

Home links
Encourage parents and carers to play a rhyming game with their children, saying, 'I hear with my little ear something that rhymes with...'.

Silly sentences

Stepping Stone
Show awareness of rhyme and alliteration.

Early Learning Goal
Use their phonic knowledge to write simple regular words and make phonetically plausible attempts at more complex words.

Group size
Any size.

What you need
Just the children.

Preparation
If you wish, make lists of suitable topics (humorous ideas work well) and related alliterative words to aid you in supporting this activity.

What to do
■ Seat the children in a circle and take your place among them.
■ Explain that you are all going to make up some silly sentences, and that lots of the words in the sentences will begin with the same sound.
■ Choose a topic such as 'Animals and clothes' and tell the children what the sentences will be about.
■ Say that you will start by telling them a silly sentence, and suggest, for example, 'Slithery snakes slip into smelly socks'.
■ Go around the circle, inviting each child to make up a silly sentence on the chosen topic.
■ Allow younger children to contribute just one word to a sentence, and build the sentence up after several children have contributed. Alternatively, cue the children by providing them with a sentence starter, for example, 'Tired tigers...'.
■ With older children, focus on a given sound, rather than a topic, and ask each child to supply a silly sentence containing lots of words that begin with the chosen sound.

More ideas
■ Read *Fox in Socks* by Dr Seuss (Collins) and ask the children to try out some of the tongue-twisters from the book.
■ Create 'mad meals' by giving the children plain paper plates and asking them to stick on pictures of foods that begin with the same sound. Use drawings or pictures cut from magazines.

Other curriculum areas
PSED Ask each child to describe the person next to them in the circle. Tell them that they must say something nice and must choose a word that starts with the same sound as the person's name, for example, 'Katy is kind' or 'Sam is smiley'.

CD Encourage the children to paint pictures of items that begin with an 'r' sound in red, others that begin with a 'b' sound in blue, and so on. Display the paintings in sound groups.

Home links
Ask parents and carers to play 'I went to the shops and bought some...', with their children and themselves taking turns to add another item that begins with the same sound to the shopping list.

Rhyming 'Snap!'

What to do

■ Explain to the children that they are going to help to make some cards, which they will then be able to use in a game.

■ Provide each child with one of the cue cards that shows both a picture and a word. Check that each child is clear about what the picture shows and what the word beneath it says.

■ Give each child a second card, explaining that the word for this picture rhymes with the one that they already have. Explain that the end of the two words sounds exactly the same, and that only the beginning of the words sounds different.

■ Ask the children to write the word for the second picture on that card. Tell them that the first letter of the word will be different from the word on the cue card, but that the rest of the word will be exactly the same, because it sounds the same.

■ Repeat the above procedure for the remaining two cards of each set.

■ When the cards are completed, explain the rules of 'Snap!' to the children, telling them that they must name each picture as they turn it over. Say that they must listen carefully for two words that rhyme and use the cards to play the game.

■ With younger children, write the initial letter of each new word on the card, and ask them to copy the end of the word from the cue card.

■ Encourage older children to work together to make additional sets of four rhyming cards to add to their game.

More ideas

■ Read rhymes to the children, missing out the rhyming word and asking them to supply it.

■ With a larger group of children, give one of the rhyming cards to each child and ask them to hunt out the others in their rhyming 'family' by walking around and showing their cards.

Other curriculum areas

KUW Teach the children some weather rhymes and ask them for a rhyme that matches the weather on any given day.

PD Use action rhymes to help the children to practise their co-ordination skills.

Stepping Stone
Continue a rhyming string.

Early Learning Goal
Use their phonic knowledge to write simple regular words and make phonetically plausible attempts at more complex words.

Group size
Three children.

What you need
The photocopiable sheet 'Find the rhyme' on page 88; thin card; glue; scissors; pencils.

Preparation
Copy the photocopiable sheet on to thin card. Cut around the individual pictures.

Home links
Ask parents and carers to read rhymes to their children and to encourage them to join in.

Price labels

Early Learning Goal
Use their phonic knowledge to write simple regular words and make phonetically plausible attempts at more complex words.

Group size
Four children.

What you need
Thin card; scissors; pencils; items for the shop, such as a cup, pen, bag and tin.

Preparation
Cut 10cm squares of card and fold them in half to make labels that will stand up.

Home links
Ask parents and carers to help their children to make labels for shelves and toy-boxes in their rooms, to remind them where everything goes.

What to do
■ Explain to the children that they are going to make price labels for a play shop.

■ Give each child an item for the shop and a label. Ask them to write the name of the item on the label.

■ Explain that it will help them to spell the word if they say it slowly and listen for each sound. Tell them that each name has three sounds and that they will need to write one letter for each sound. Check that they can hear the three sounds and that they know the letter to write for each sound.

■ Ask the child to add a price for the item.

■ Help younger children by sounding out the word for them and by writing a model of the word for them to copy.

■ Encourage older children to try to write more complex labels. Show them how to use dashes to write sounds or parts of words that they are not sure of.

More ideas
■ Lay out three letters of a word, written on card, in the wrong order. Ask the children to work together to unjumble the word.

■ Start word collections by writing appropriate endings on containers, for example, '-ag' on a bag, '-in' on a tin, and so on. Give the children cards and help them to build a word by writing one letter and then the ending. Add the word to the collection in the correct container.

Other curriculum areas
CD Spread paint on a smooth, wipe-clean surface and ask the children to write simple words in the paint, using their fingers. Lay a piece of paper on the paint and gently pass a hand over it, to take a word print.

KUW Help the children to make greetings cards for special days and encourage them to write simple messages, for example, 'To Mum and Dad'.

Communication, language and literacy

With these ideas, the children will develop the skills that they need for early reading. Some of the activities provide the opportunity to take an active part in storytelling, while others encourage the children to attend to the detail of words.

Tell the story

What to do

■ Tell the children that you are going to look at a picture book together. Show them the book and explain that there are no words in it but that you are all going to tell the story, by looking at the pictures and working out what is happening.

■ Turn to the first page and cue the children in by saying, 'This is a story about...?'.

■ Make up the story for the first few pages, referring back to the pictures with phrases such as, 'Look, you can see that here'.

■ After a few pages, say, 'I wonder what happens next? Can you tell me?' and hand over the storytelling to one of the children.

■ Make sure that each child has the opportunity to contribute to the story.

■ Help younger children by asking them specific questions about the illustrations.

■ Allow older children to begin storytelling independently without modelling the first few pages.

More ideas

■ Look at posters (or use wrapping paper with detailed overall pictures) and encourage the children to examine the pictures over a period of time and to talk about what they can see. Then hold a group session to compare the children's versions of the poster story. Change the poster regularly.

■ Ask the children to choose their favourite picture in a book and to say what they especially like about it.

Stepping Stone
Show interest in illustrations and print in books.

Early Learning Goal
Explore and experiment with sounds, words and texts.
■
Group size
Four to six children.
■
What you need
A copy of *Sunshine* or *Moonshine* both by Jan Ormerod (Penguin – out of print) or any picture picture book without text.

Other curriculum areas

KUW Look at a variety of books with the children, to explore what illustrations can tell us. Show them, for example, how some pictures help us to understand the story, others tell us how things work, and some can teach us about how people live in different countries.

CD After reading a story to the children, encourage them to paint a picture to illustrate one part of the story. Display their pictures with captions from the story.

Home links
Explain to parents and carers how important illustrations in books are for young children. Encourage them to discuss the pictures with their children, when they are reading to them.

Communication, language and literacy

What if?

Stepping Stone
Suggest how the story might end.

Early Learning Goal
Explore and experiment with sounds, words and texts.

Group size
Any size.

What you need
A copy of *Dogger* by Shirley Hughes (Red Fox) or any story-book in which the outcome depends on one particular event.

Home links
Suggest to parents and carers that, sometimes, when reading stories to their children, they pause at exciting points to ask the child what they think will happen next.

What to do

■ Read the story of *Dogger,* or the story of your choice, to the children.

■ When you reach the parts of the book where events could go one way or the other, pause to ask questions. *Dogger* offers several possibilities: 'Will Dave get back to the stall in time with his money?', 'Is the little girl going to agree to sell Dogger back to Dave?' or 'What do you think Bella decided to do?'.

■ At the end of the story, suggest to the children that the story could have ended differently. Ask what they think would have happened if Dave had not seen Dogger on the stall, or if Bella had not offered to give the little girl her teddy.

■ Invite the children to tell you which ending they prefer.

■ Prompt younger children with questions to help them to suggest alternative endings.

■ Ask older children to pinpoint where in the story things could have happened very differently.

More ideas

■ Make a collection of pictures from magazines that 'tell a story'. Have regular storytelling sessions when the children choose a picture and say what they think happened just before and just after the picture was taken.

■ Start the day in your setting with 'Guess what Teddy will choose'. Tell the children what the group teddy is feeling like, saying, for example, 'Teddy is feeling very bouncy. He wants to swing and climb. Where do you think he will choose to play?'.

Other curriculum areas

MD Encourage prediction skills by providing the children with a set of containers of varying size and shape. Ask them to fill each one with the same quantity of water and to predict whether it will fit into the container.

KUW Place a collection of everyday objects in a bag. Ask the children to put their hand in the bag and to guess what one object is by feeling it. Encourage them to describe what it feels like before they guess what it is. Check whether their predictions are correct.

Sound story

What to do

■ Read *Peace at Last* to the children.

■ Explain to the children that you are going to read the story again, but that some parts will be missing. Say that all the missing parts will be sounds. Tell the children that you would like them to fill in the missing sounds and that you will hold up pictures to remind them of what to say.

■ Hold up the picture of the cuckoo clock and explain that, for example, when they see this you

want them to say, 'Tick-tock, Tick-tock. Cuckoo! Cuckoo!'. Read the story again, holding up the cue cards for each sound effect, in turn.

■ Help younger children by showing them all the cards before the second reading and reminding them of what they should say each time.

■ Challenge older children to help you to tell a funny version of the story by giving the wrong sound effects.

More ideas

■ Help the children to understand that their own experiences can form the basis of stories. Make a cardboard 'book cover' with an acetate pocket on the front. Slip pictures or titles into this pocket and show the 'book' to introduce the children as they tell their 'story'. Use an animal picture to cue the children's stories of 'My pet', for example. Write up their stories.

■ Display a story-book together with appropriate dressing-up clothes and props that the children can use to act out that story in a special corner. Change the book and props regularly.

Other curriculum areas

MD Tell number stories by stacking up some bricks and telling a story about a little girl who built a tower. Ask the children to say how many bricks she added each time. Show how her baby brother knocked it down, asking how many bricks were left.

PD As you tell a familiar story, encourage the children to act out the movements of one particular character.

Behaving badly

Stepping Stone
Begin to be aware of the way stories are structured.

Early Learning Goal
Retell narratives in the correct sequence, drawing on language patterns of stories.

Group size
Any size.

What you need
A copy of *Where the Wild Things Are* by Maurice Sendak (Red Fox) or any picture book in which a central child character misbehaves.

Home links
Explain to parents and carers the important role they can play in encouraging their children in reading by making time to read regularly to their children.

What to do
■ Tell the children that you are going to read them a story about a child who behaves rather naughtily.

■ Read *Where the Wild Things Are* or your chosen story to the children.

■ Talk about Max, or your main character, inviting the children to tell you whether they think that he enjoyed being naughty at first. Ask, for example, if Max got fed up of being a 'wild thing' in the end. Talk about Max finding his supper waiting for him. Do the children think that his mum had forgiven him for being naughty?

■ Ask the children if any of them have ever been naughty. Tell them that you would like them to tell their story, saying that you would like to know what they did, what happened to them and how things worked out in the end.

■ With younger children, draw attention to the expressions on Max's face in the pictures to help them to understand what he was feeling at different points in the story.

■ Ask older children if they can think of other stories in which children or other characters have misbehaved.

Other curriculum areas
MD Draw simple story-sequence pictures on cards, for example, a sequence of a seed, a shoot and a plant, and ask the children to arrange the pictures in order to make a story.

CD Provide the children with 'naughty' puppets and ask each child to help their puppet tell the story of 'The naughtiest thing I have ever done'.

More ideas
■ Provide ample opportunities for the children to recount events that have happened to them. Give them the status of 'storyteller' by having a special hat, cape or badge that they wear when they are telling their story.

■ Give the children the experience of listening to stories with repeated scenes, such as 'The Enormous Turnip' (Traditional), so that the children can take over the storytelling in turn.

Communication, language and literacy

Which way?

What to do

■ Explain to the children that you are going to think about how books work.

■ Show the children a detailed illustration from *Peepo*, or your chosen book, and ask them to tell you what is happening.

■ Turn to another illustration, but this time hold the book upside-down. Ask if it is difficult to work out what is happening. Remind the children that we must hold the book the right way up when we are reading.

■ Start reading the story from the last page backwards. Ask the children if it makes sense. Explain that we must start at the front of a book and read from top to bottom, left to right. Read a page correctly, tracking the text with your finger.

■ Explain that writing works differently in some countries. Show the children the Chinese writing and explain that in China writing is read from top to bottom but from right to left.

■ With younger children, omit the sample of Chinese writing and focus on the activities with your chosen book.

■ Ask older children to try to write their names from the top to the bottom of a piece of paper and to see if it is harder to recognise it.

More ideas

■ Take photographs of everyday objects from different angles and ask the children to guess what the items are.

■ Make simple books with the children, using their own drawings. Scribe captions for them and let them design covers. Encourage them to 'read' the books to each other.

Other curriculum areas

PSED Play 'Chinese whispers' with the children to illustrate how important it is that we understand messages correctly, whether they are spoken or written.

KUW Show the children what happens when you turn letters such as 'd' and 'p', or 'm' and 'w', upside-down. Explain how important it is to write letters the correct way, so that people can understand what we write.

Stepping Stone
Hold books the correct way up and turn pages.

Early Learning Goal
Know that print carries meaning and, in English, is read from left to right and top to bottom.

■

Group size
Any size.

■

What you need
An example of Chinese writing; book with detailed illustrations such as *Peepo* by Janet and Allan Ahlberg (Picture Puffin).

■

Preparation
Make enlarged photocopies of the sample of Chinese writing.

Home links
Ask parents and carers to help their children be aware of how books work, by letting them open story-books at the starting-point, hold the books while listening and turn the pages.

Word riddles

Early Learning Goal
Read a range of familiar and common words and simple sentences independently.

Group size
Four children.

What you need
Access to a computer; thin card.

Preparation
Type out the words 'sun', 'cat', 'man', 'net', 'hat', 'can', 'leg', 'jug', 'pen', 'peg', 'dog' and 'hen'. Print the words out in a large font, stick the sheet of paper on to thin card and cut out the individual word cards. Decide on simple clues for each of the 12 words, for example, 'I shine in the sky' as a clue for 'sun'. Write your clues on pieces of card.

What to do

Shuffle the word cards and deal three cards to each child. Say that they are going to play a word game. Explain that you are going to give them a clue for a word and that you want them to think about the answer to your clue, and then to look and see if they have the right word among their cards.

Shuffle the clue cards and read out the first clue. The child who has the answer card turns it over. The first one to turn over all three of their cards is the winner.

Help younger children by giving the first sound of the target word, after the clue. Draw simple pictures on the back of their cards, corresponding to the words, so that they can check a word if they are unsure.

Add extra word cards for older children.

More ideas

Include written signs in your room, such as an 'open/closed' sign in the shop corner, a library sign in the book corner, a baker's sign on the play-dough table, a swimming-pool sign on the water tray, and so on.

Make pairs of animal cards with the animal name on one card and a picture of the animal on the other. Give the cards out and ask the children to find their partners.

Home links
Explain to parents and carers that they can play an important part in helping their children to become readers, by making sure that their children see them engaged in reading. Ask them to label things around the house, such as the child's chair, room and bed with their child's name.

Other curriculum area
MD Write number words on large pieces of card. Give these out before reading number rhymes such as 'Ten in the Bed' (Traditional). Ask the children to hold up the correct number word and say it when you stop reading. Pause in your reading when you reach the number words.

Follow the recipe

What to do
■ Give each child a recipe sheet and tell them that they are going to make some cakes by following the instructions.
■ Read through the ingredients with the children. Help them to collect together everything they need and share the melted chocolate equally between four bowls.
■ Ensure that the children carry out each step of the recipe safely.
■ With younger children, work through the recipe together, allowing each child to carry out a small task. Use the illustrations to help them to understand what is required.
■ Let older children perform tasks more independently and allow them to choose one of the 'special' ingredients to add.

More ideas
■ Ask the children to contribute to an 'information' display. Collect recipes, knitting patterns, cinema programmes, bus timetables, newspaper advertisements and so on. Talk about the different types of information that these items give us.

Other curriculum areas
PSED Make up a group recipe for 'A happy day', including things such as smiling at someone, saying something nice to someone and being helpful. Invite the group to follow the recipe for one day and to talk about how the day went.

MD Ask the children to create 'number recipes'. Make sheets that have headings such as 'To make 6 you need...?'. Help the children to find different 'recipes' using DUPLO blocks, such as 'two blue and four red' or 'three green and three yellow'.

■ Set up an 'Information point' by inviting the children to come to the adult on duty to ask questions about things that they would like to know. Write the questions down and try to find out answers within 24 hours, showing the children the information source that you consulted.

Garden safari

Stepping Stone
Know that information can be retrieved from books and computers.

Early Learning Goal
Show an understanding of how information can be found in non-fiction texts to answer questions about where, who, why and how.

Group size
Any size.

What you need
A selection of simple information books about minibeasts; clipboards; paper; pencils; adult helpers to support small groups.

Preparation
Decide on a venue such as a garden or park for your safari.

Home links
Ask parents and carers to respond positively to their children's questions, and to suggest that they try to find out answers together by looking in books.

What to do
■ Tell the children that they are going on a safari to hunt for minibeasts. Suggest that they look for woodlice, spiders, bees, worms and so on.
■ Ask the children to draw all the minibeasts that they see.
■ Explore your chosen venue. Invite helpers to talk with the children about the minibeasts that they see. Encourage the children to look under stones and amongst foliage. Make sure that they always return any minibeasts to the place that they were found.
■ Back indoors explain to the children that you are all going to find out some more about the minibeasts that they discovered.

■ Ask the children, in turn, to show a drawing and say what they found. Look up information about that minibeast in one of the books and share it with the children.
■ With younger children, make explicit what you are doing as you look for information. Let them talk about what they notice in the illustrations.
■ Let older children explore the books for themselves and bring to you any information that they can find to read together.

More ideas
■ Show the children that they can store the information that they have discovered by making a book about their safari (see the activity 'Safari book' on page 68).
■ Look through an information book with the children. Afterwards, ask how many of them have learned something that they did not know before.

Other curriculum areas
PSED Promote the children's interests in the cultures of other children in the group by exploring appropriate information books together.

KUW Ask the children if there are subjects that they would like to find out more about. Explore the book collection or a library together to see if there are books on that subject.

Who, where, why?

What to do

■ Tell the children that they are going to help you to make up a story. Explain that the first thing that they must do is to choose a main character. Say that this means deciding who the story will be about.

■ Hold up the soft toys in turn, asking questions such as, 'Shall we make a teddy our main character, or a rabbit, or a dog?'. Decide on a name for the main character.

■ Now show the pictures of the different places and ask the children to consider where this character lives.

■ Suggest that, one day, this character decides to go on a journey. Show the pictures again and ask where the children think he goes. Once this is decided, ask why he is making the journey and what happens when he gets there.

■ Support younger children by asking specific questions to help them to structure the story.

■ With older children, use the other soft toys from your selection as props to introduce other characters that the main character meets during the course of the story.

More ideas

■ Hold an 'Important people's tea party' and ask the children to each come dressed as the main character from their favourite book. Make place cards in the characters' names, and ask each 'guest' to say why they are so important in their particular book.

■ Play 'Guess the character', giving a clue for a character in a fairy story, such as 'I am a little girl who saved my granny from a wolf', and asking the children to guess who you are.

Other curriculum areas

CD Ask the children to each paint a picture of the main character from their favourite book.

PSED Invite the children to retell stories as if they are main characters, for example, Goldilocks or the wolf who blew the little pigs' houses down. Then discuss how the other characters in the stories might have felt.

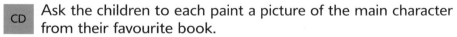

Stepping Stone
Begin to be aware of the way stories are structured.

Early Learning Goal
Show an understanding of the elements of stories, such as main character, sequence of events and openings.

■

Group size
Any size.

■

What you need
A selection of soft toys; pictures of different environments, such as a house, garden, town, country and seaside, cut from magazines.

Home links
Suggest that parents and carers might like to set aside time for storytelling sessions, making up simple stories in which their child feature as the main character.

Right or wrong?

Stepping Stone
Understand the concept of a word.

Early Learning Goal
Read a range of familiar and common words and simple sentences independently.

Group size
Two to four children.

What you need
A copy of the photocopiable sheet 'Word detectives' on page 91 for each child; pencils.

What to do
■ Tell the children that they are going to play at being word detectives.
■ Show them the photocopiable sheet. Explain that one of the sentences says something that is true about each picture, and that the other sentence says something that is not true. Tell the children that they have to decide which one is true.
■ Point out that the sentences look very alike but that one word is different in each one. This word makes the sentence true or not. Ask them to look very carefully and to try to work out which is true. Help with any words that the children cannot read. Tell them to tick the box by the true sentence.
■ Ask younger children to only work out which words in the sentences are different. Then read both sentences to them, so that they can decide which is true.
■ Let older children read the sentences independently.

More ideas
■ Play 'Hunt the word'. Choose a key word such as 'and', 'the' or 'is'. Show the word to the children and tell them what it is. Enlarge and copy a piece of newsprint and ask the children to hunt for their key word in the print, and to circle it in red each time they find it.

Home links
Suggest a game in which the carer writes four categories, such as 'colour', 'animal', 'food' and 'vehicle', on pieces of card. They then turn the cards face down and take turns with their child to pick up a card and then say a word in that category. For example, if they turn over 'colour', they might say 'red'.

Other curriculum areas
CD Choose five objects from the room. Show one at a time to the children and ask them for words that describe it. Write the words on cards and count them to see which object 'won' the most words.

MD Help the children to understand that symbols such as '+' and '-' are alternatives for words. Use real objects for simple addition and subtraction calculations, and cards with the maths symbol on one side and a word on the other. Turn the card to show the word as you 'read' the sum.

The activities in this chapter provide practice in essential mark-making skills, together with purposeful opportunities for the children to write their names and to attempt further writing for a variety of purposes.

Taking orders

What to do
■ Show the 'café' to the children. Explain to them that they are going to pretend to be ordering food and drinks there. Remind them that there is usually a menu in a café, from which customers choose what they would like. Show the children the prepared menu and talk through the items listed.

■ Ask the children to decide which two children will act as waiters, and give these children aprons to wear and pads and pencils to write down the orders.

■ Invite the customers to take their seats, and join in with the game yourself, as another customer. Provide support with reading the menu and with writing the orders, if necessary. Accept any attempt at making marks or writing words to record the orders.

■ With younger children, provide the waiters with extra copies of menus, rather than writing pads, so that they can just tick the items that are ordered.

■ Encourage older children to write initial letters or to try writing words for the items ordered.

More ideas
■ Set up a hospital for dolls and teddies, using shoeboxes as beds. Attach paper 'charts' to the ends of beds with bulldog clips and encourage the children to fill them in.

■ Ask a child to lay a trail of chalk crosses (or pencil crosses on pieces of paper) and to hide, letting the other children follow the trail in order to find them.

Other curriculum areas
PD Hold jumping trials, encouraging the children to try to jump further on each of three tries. Mark their jumps with chalk marks on the floor.

MD Weigh dolls and teddies on a balance scale, using bricks as weights. Ask the children to fill in weight charts by drawing a picture of the toy and a square for each brick weight needed.

Stepping Stone
Draw and paint, sometimes giving meanings to marks.

Early Learning Goal
Attempt writing for different purposes, using features of different forms such as lists, stories and instructions.
■
Group size
Six children.
■
What you need
Four copies of a simple illustrated menu (extra copies if the waiters are younger children); two tables; five chairs; play crockery and food; two aprons; writing pads; pencils.
■
Preparation
Make up a simple menu illustrating each item and photocopy it on to thin card. Set up a café scenario, placing a menu on each of the tables.

Home links
Explain to parents and carers that they should praise any attempt that their children make to write, including simply making marks or pretend writing.

Writing robot

Stepping Stone
Draw and paint, sometimes giving meanings to marks.

Early Learning Goal
Use their phonic knowledge to write simple regular words and make phonically plausible attempts at more complex words.

Group size
Four to six children.

What you need
Paper; pencils; colouring crayons or felt-tipped pens.

What to do

■ Ask the children to suggest some reasons why we might need to write. If necessary, cue them in to ideas such as letters, lists, cheques, forms and so on.

■ Tell the children that you are having a very busy time, because you have a lot of writing to do. Say that it would be really wonderful if you could have some help with all your work. Suggest that the children design a robot for you that would be able to do lots of the writing.

■ Discuss with the children what the robot might look like and what it might need, for example, pens, ink, paper, envelopes and so on.

■ Give the children paper and pencils to each design a robot, then move around, discussing their designs with them. Suggest that it would help you to know how the robot works and ask if they could write names on some of the parts.

■ Accept any marks or attempts at writing that are made by younger children. Scribe specific words for them if they ask for this help.

■ Encourage older children to try to write a few sentences about how the robot works.

More ideas

■ Set up a 'post office' role-play corner and provide envelopes, paper, scales to weigh parcels, rubber stamps and an ink pad. Wrap empty boxes with brown paper to make parcels.

■ Provide a simple outline plan of your setting. Explain it to the children, then let them work in pairs, with one child hiding a 'treasure' and marking its position on the map for the other to find.

Home links
Ask parents and carers to talk with their children about any drawings and paintings that they produce at home, and to help them to write titles or captions on their work.

Other curriculum areas

KUW Set up a sundial using an upturned flowerpot with a garden cane projecting through the hole. Ask the children to mark the position of the stick shadow with chalk at various times through the day.

MD Make a group height chart and let the children mark on height lines and names for each other.

Communication, language and literacy

Don't forget the...

Stepping Stone
Ascribe meanings to marks.

Early Learning Goal
Attempt writing for different purposes, using features of different forms such as lists, stories and instructions.

Group size
Four to six children.

What you need
Small suitcase or bag; five items for a holiday, such as a beach towel, shorts, T-shirt, trainers and cap; paper; pencils.

Preparation
Pack the holiday items in the case. Make a list of essential items for a holiday.

What to do
■ Show the children your case and explain that you are getting ready for a short holiday. Say that you have already packed some things that you will need. Open the case and show the items to the children. Then tell them that you have made a list of other things that you could not manage without.

■ Explain that you will probably be able to buy anything that you forget to pack in a shop. Wonder out loud what you would do if you were going somewhere without shops, for example, if you were going to the moon for a holiday. Say that you would have to remember to take everything with you.

■ Ask the children what they would pack to take to the moon. Accept some ideas, then suggest to the children that they write a list of what they would take. Give them pencils and paper. Discuss their lists as they are written.

■ Allow younger children to make marks, use pretend writing or write initial letters, and to supplement these with drawings.

■ Challenge older children to list only the five most important items that they could not do without.

More ideas
■ Encourage the children to set up a school for toys. Show them how to make a register of pupils. Suggest that they teach the toys how to write.

■ Record a tape of everyday sounds such as footsteps, a tap dripping and a toilet flushing. Provide 'Lotto' sheets with simple pictures representing the corresponding activities on them, and ask the children to tick the correct pictures as they hear the sounds.

Home links
Encourage parents to make lists with their children to prepare for a shopping trip, a holiday or of friends to invite to parties.

Other curriculum areas
PSED Make a communal list of 'Things that make us smile'. Display the list, together with the children's illustrations of the 'smile triggers'.

KUW Set up a weather chart for the children to fill in each day. Use very simple symbols and/or words, such as:

Teddy bears' party

Early Learning Goal
Write their own names.

Group size
Four to six children.

What you need
Scissors; pencils.

Preparation
Use the diagrams on this page to make a simple place card for each child and a hat for each teddy. Draw out the design on to paper, then copy it on to card.

What to do
■ Explain to the children that you are going to hold a 'Teddy bears' tea party' and that you want them all to bring their own bears.
■ Tell them that they are going to make some party hats and some place cards for their bears, so that they will know where they have to sit.
■ Give each child a template for the hat and the place card. Explain that you want them to write their own name on each of these, so that their bear will know where to sit and will have the hat that they have decorated.
■ When they have written their name on both the place card and hat, ask each child to cut both of these out. Then suggest that they decorate the hat with their own design.
■ Help younger children by giving them a dotted-line version of their name to write over.
■ Ask older children to write an invitation to the party for their bear.

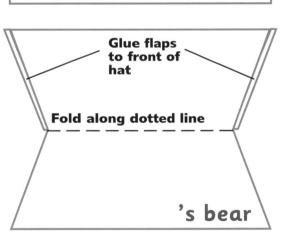

Cut along solid line

Fold along dotted line

's bear

Glue flaps to front of hat

Fold along dotted line

's bear

More ideas
■ Have a large sheet of paper available for the children to sign or tick themselves in on arrival at the party.
■ Use a whiteboard, blackboard or pinboard as a 'News board' and ask the children to put their names on it if they have some news that they would like to share. Choose names from the board at circle time.

Home links
Encourage parents and carers to involve their children in 'signing' letters, cards and birthday invitations. Explain that, if necessary, the children can just make a mark, and the adult can add the name beneath it.

Other curriculum areas
CD Read three nursery rhymes. Provide three sheets of paper, with the name of one main character and a drawing on each, for example, a toy lamb for Bo Peep, or a plant for Mary Mary. Ask the children to vote for the character that they would like to invite to their party by writing their names.

PD Draw one large arrow on each of four large pieces of card: one pointing up, one pointing down, one pointing right and the other left. With the children facing you, hold up a card to indicate which way they must move: forwards, backwards, right or left. Vary the movements using steps, jumps, hops and so on.

Frog or dog?

What to do

■ Read *A Fly Went by* to the children. Talk with them about their favourite part of the story and their favourite animals in it.

■ Tell the children that you would like them to choose their favourite part of the chase from the story. Ask them to draw or paint the two animals from that part of the story. If possible, encourage different children to choose different sections of the story.

■ When the children have finished their pictures, say that you would like them to write the names of the animals that they have drawn underneath their pictures.

■ Provide younger children with models of the animal names to copy.

■ Ask older children to try to arrange the finished pictures in the order of the story. Display the pictures as a frieze and use it as a stimulus for retelling the story.

More ideas

■ Set up a den with a blanket thrown over a table. Provide a torch, pencils, paper and a box, such as an old cash box or a shoebox with a slit in the lid, to leave secret messages in.

■ Show the children an example of Chinese writing (see the activity 'Which way?' page 53). Provide paper, brushes and black paint, and let them experiment with some Chinese writing, working from top to bottom and right to left.

Stepping Stone
Ascribe meanings to marks.

Early Learning Goal
Use their phonic knowledge to write simple regular words and make phonically plausible attempts at more complex words.

■

Group size
Any size.

■

What you need
A copy of *A Fly Went by* by Michael McClintock (Collins); paper; pencils; paint.

Home links
Explain to parents and carers that their children's writing skills will develop over a long period, and that they may miss out letters in words or confuse different letters. Suggest that they always comment positively about their children's attempts at writing.

Other curriculum areas

PSED At Divali, show the children pictures of mendhi hand patterns and talk about their meaning. Ask each child to make a handprint in paint and, when it is dry, to decorate it with their own design.

CD Draw animal symbols (see illustration) on to pieces of card. When singing 'Old Macdonald Had a Farm' (Traditional) hold them up in turn to indicate the next animal in the song. Ask the children to make symbols for other animals.

Follow the instructions

Stepping Stone
Ascribe meanings to marks.

Early Learning Goal
Use their phonic knowledge to write simple regular words and make phonically plausible attempts at more complex words.

■

Group size
Two to three children.

■

What you need
A selection of small boxes such as snack-bar boxes and trifle-sponge boxes; scissors; glue; glue brushes; paper; colouring pencils; pencils.

■

Preparation
Make a puppet in advance as a finished example (see illustration, top right).

Home links
Encourage parents and carers to leave simple notes for their children, asking for help with tasks, for example, 'Please help lay the table'.

What to do
■ Say to the children that you are going to show them how to make a puppet.
■ Choose a box and re-glue the opened end. Half-way along the box, make a cut around three sides, leaving one side intact. Fold the box in half across the intact side, to form a mouth. (See illustration, right.)
■ Cut pieces of paper to cover the box. Spread the box surfaces with glue and stick the paper on.
■ Draw eyes, nostrils, teeth and so on to create the head of a real or imaginary creature.
■ Tell the children that they are going to write down the instructions, to help them to make their own puppets.
■ Encourage them to keep their instructions very simple, for example, 'cut', 'fold', 'stick' and 'draw'. Let the children make their puppets.
■ Scribe for younger children, asking them to add illustrations.
■ Encourage older children to write simple sentences.

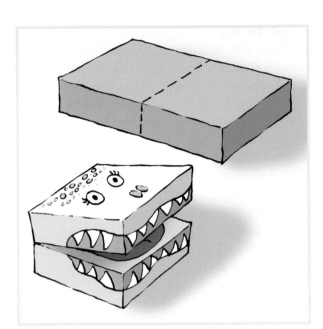

More ideas
■ Ask the children to draw a simple map of their route to your setting, and to put a cross on the most interesting thing that they pass.
■ Use chalk to draw a target with a bull's eye on a wall. Invite the children to throw beanbags at the bull's eye and to score hits, using a different coloured tally mark for each child.

Other curriculum areas
MD Draw a caterpillar face on one paper plate. Write one numeral in the well of five other plates (or more) and lay the plates out in sequence. Give the children plates with coloured dots on them, corresponding to the numerals, and ask them to place the correct number of dots over each numeral.

KUW Draw simple animal tracks (see illustration below) on pieces of paper. Provide the relevant toy animals and ask the children to match each animal to the tracks. Invite them to draw more tracks to add to the game.

A day in the life of...

What to do

■ Show the children the photographs. Explain that you would like to use them for a display or an album, and that you want people to know who is in each photo. Say that you would like them to write something about the photos.

■ Put out a selection of photos and invite the children to each find one of themselves. Ask them to say a short sentence about what they were doing in the photo. Give them a piece of paper and a pencil. Provide a model of a sentence starter such as 'This is...' and encourage them to copy this, adding their name and something about what they were doing.

■ Ask younger children simply to add their names or edit their sentences, inviting the child to read back what they have written and writing an edited version beneath their efforts.

■ Encourage older children to attempt their own sentences, without starter cues.

More ideas

■ Make a group alphabet book using photos of the children. Dress them up as characters to illustrate some letters, for example, **a**stronauts and **c**lowns, then provide plates of wobbly jelly for them to hold for '**j**uggling **j**elly', or dress them in zipped jackets for '**z**ipping up'. Write captions and let the children in the photos add their names underneath.

■ Make 'My family' zigzag books, in which the children draw members of their own families and try to write the names beneath their drawings.

Other curriculum areas

PSED Make 'All about me' books. Let each child write their name on a cover and provide pages with headings such as 'My favourite colour', 'My favourite food' and so on. Praise each child's attempts to fill in their book, using drawings, marks or writing.

MD Provide the children with matchboxes, with a numeral written on the outside. Ask them to look for objects that will fit in the box and to put the correct number inside each box.

Early Learning Goal
Write their own names and other things such as labels and captions.

■

Group size
Four to six children.

■

What you need
Photographs of each child in the group, engaged in any everyday activity at your setting; paper; pencils.

■

Preparation
Take photographs of all the children engaged in everyday activities. Have the photos developed and printed.

Home links
Ask parents and carers to help their children to create photo albums of their own activities, and support them in writing captions for the photos.

Please reply

Early Learning Goal
Attempt writing for different purposes, using features of different forms such as lists, stories and instructions.

Group size
Four children.

What you need
Paper; pencils; envelopes; group post-box, made from any cardboard box and painted red; group teddy bear; elastic band.

Preparation
Place the teddy near the post-box, equipped with a pencil (fixed to a paw with an elastic band) and a half-written letter.
Tell the group that Teddy likes writing letters and may write to them.
Write secret, short notes, signed by Teddy, to individual children. Include a question.
Place the notes, secretly, in the post-box.

What to do
■ Check the post-box, in front of the children. Call over those who have received letters.
■ Let them open their letters and help them to read them. Suggest that they write a note back to Teddy, answering his questions.
■ Provide each child with paper and an envelope. Model the writing of 'Dear Teddy' for them.
■ Talk with the children about what they want to write, before they attempt their letter. Praise all attempts, from scribble to emergent writing. Assist the children with addressing the envelopes, and let them post their letters.
■ Support younger children by helping them to decide what they will write in their letters.
■ Encourage older children to work independently writing, posting and receiving replies from Teddy.

More ideas
■ Make a communal instruction manual for the group Teddy, detailing what he likes to eat, wear and do. Allow individual children to look after Teddy for a day, reading through the manual with them first.

■ Suggest that the children write a note to their parents and carers to request their favourite meal for the next day. Encourage them to illustrate the note with a drawing of the meal.

Home links
Encourage parents and carers to leave notes around the house, such as on a pillow or chair, for their children to find. Explain that they will stimulate their children to write replies if they include simple questions such as 'Have you had a nice day?' or 'What would you like for tea?'.

Other curriculum areas
PSED Ask the children to make a 'Have a happy day' card to send to someone they love.

KUW Help the children to make pairs of cards, one with a red letter 'y' (for 'yes') written on it, the other with a black letter 'n' (for 'no'). Play a game by making simple statements such as 'Cows miaow' and asking the children to hold up their 'y' card if this is true, or their 'n' card if it is not.

The journey of a leaf

Early Learning Goal
Begin to form simple sentences.

Group size
Any size.

What you need
Paper; pen.

Preparation
Decide on a walk where the children might observe fallen leaves, ideally in autumn or on a windy day.

What to do

■ Take the children for a walk and point out leaves that have fallen or been blown from the trees.

■ Back indoors, wonder aloud about how far leaves get blown by the wind and where they go. Suggest that you all make up a story about the journey of a leaf. Say that you will write the story down.

■ Ask the children to contribute ideas for the places that the leaf visits and what happens to it. Write down each contribution on a different piece of paper, drawing attention to individual words as you write.

■ 'Accidentally' mix up the pieces of paper. Encourage the children to retell the story in the right order, so that you can sort out the papers and read the story to them.

■ Help younger children by suggesting the places that the leaf visits and asking them what it might see there.

■ Let older children attempt to write down their own contributions. Piece the story together from these.

More ideas

■ Tell the children that visitors are coming from another planet. Ask them to make labels for items in the room, to help them to understand our language. Dress up an adult as a space visitor and read the labels.

■ Help the children to make guidebooks for their homes using pictures from magazines, or drawings, and inviting the children to try to write the names of the rooms beneath the pictures.

Home links
Ask parents and carers to make sure that their children see them engaged in writing letters, lists or other messages. Tell them to say to their children what they are writing out loud, word by word.

Other curriculum areas

CD Ask the children to imagine some of the sounds that the leaf might hear on its journey. As they make suggestions, write the sound words on large cards. Retell the story, holding up the sound word cards and asking the children to make the sounds effects.

PSED Make simple badges from card discs, safety-pins and sticky tape. Write on words such as 'kindness', 'helpfulness' and 'sharing'. Award a few badges a day, talking about the words that are written on them. Let the children fill in blank badges to award to one another.

Safari book

Stepping Stone
Use writing as a
means of recording.

**Early Learning
Goal**
Begin to form simple
sentences,
sometimes using
punctuation.

■

Group size
Four children.

■

What you need
A4 paper folded and
stapled to make A5
booklets; pencils;
colouring pencils.

■

Preparation
Carry out the activity
'Garden safari' on
page 56. Photocopy
a prepared master
booklet for younger
children.

Home links
Encourage parents
and carers to talk
about family outings
and to sometimes
scribe their child's
'story' of what they
have seen and done.

What to do

■ Tell the children that they are going to make books about the minibeasts that they found on their safari. Give out the booklets and provide a model of a 'Minibeasts' title for them to copy on to their front covers. Ask each child to write their name underneath as the 'author'.

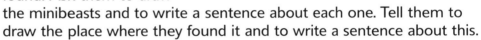

■ Suggest that they use one page for each minibeast that they found. Ask them to draw the minibeasts and to write a sentence about each one. Tell them to draw the place where they found it and to write a sentence about this.

■ Help the children as they work, providing spellings or helping by scribing, as necessary.

■ Supply younger children with booklets with a ready-prepared format to be filled in. Use sentence openers such as 'I found a...' and 'I found it...'. Encourage the use of drawings and initial letters.

■ Invite older children to add anything else that they know about each minibeast.

More ideas

■ Provide 'diary' sheets with outline pictures of a television, a plate and a person. Ask the children to write something about a programme that they watched, something that they ate and someone that they met, on the appropriate pictures.

■ Use a teddy as a measure and ask the children to find out, for example, how many teddies long the table is. Provide a sheet with sentences for the children to complete, such as 'The... is... teddies long.'

Other curriculum areas

KUW Experiment with things that float and sink, such as a grape and an apple, or a feather and a piece of wood. Give the children a cutaway diagram of a bowl of water and ask them to write the names of things that sink at the bottom and of those that float at the top. Scribe for them if necessary.

CD Encourage the children to create stories with play figures. Offer to write the book of their story and ask them to draw the illustrations.

This chapter provides activities that are designed to promote the large and small movement skills that underlie handwriting. The graded activities progress through to the finer manipulative skills that will enable the children to hold and move a pencil with ease.

Good shot

What to do
■ Place the pyramid of boxes on a table. Mark a line with chalk or tape on the floor about a metre away, and pile up the paper balls by the line.
■ Explain to the children that they are going to take it in turns to throw the balls of paper at the boxes. Tell them that the idea is to try to get one ball in any of the boxes.
■ Ask the children to stand behind the line to throw their paper balls. Let them take it in turns to throw a ball at the boxes.
■ Allow younger children to stand nearer to the boxes and to throw the balls using two hands.
■ Set older children the goal of getting one ball into each of the boxes.

More ideas
■ Place a series of containers with different-sized openings on the floor and ask the children to throw a rolled-up sock into the containers. Award points for each hit, with higher scores for containers that are smaller.
■ Make skittles from plastic drinks bottles with 5cm of water in the bottom and use a large foam ball to knock them down.

Other curriculum areas
PD Tie a ball of screwed-up newspaper to a length of string. Tape the other end of the string to a door frame, so that the ball hangs down. Provide two children with rolled-up newspapers to hit the ball back and forwards to each other.

KUW Ask the children to hold a large container with both hands to pour sand or water into other containers from different heights.

Goals for the Foundation Stage

Stepping Stone
Engage in activities requiring hand–eye co-ordination.

Early Learning Goal
Use a pencil and hold it effectively to form recognisable letters, most of which are correctly formed.

Group size
Four children.

What you need
Six cardboard boxes; scrap paper or newspaper; sticky tape; table; chalk or parcel tape.

Preparation
Arrange the cardboard boxes in a pyramid, with three in the bottom row, two in the middle and one on the top, with all the openings forwards. Tape each row of boxes together for stability. Screw up scrap paper to form balls, each approximately the size of a tennis ball.

Home links
Encourage parents and carers to play throwing and catching games with their children, explaining how the development of these large movement skills will help their children to develop the smaller movement skills needed later for writing.

Follow the cat

Stepping Stone
Engage in activities requiring hand–eye co-ordination.

Early Learning Goal
Use a pencil and hold it effectively to form recognisable letters, most of which are correctly formed.

Group size
Any size.

What you need
A copy of the photocopiable sheet 'Let's go exploring' on page 92 for each child; pencils.

What to do
■ Give each child a copy of the photocopiable sheet and a pencil. Explain that the four pictures tell the story of a cat that likes to go exploring at night when everyone is asleep.
■ Tell the children that they are going to follow the cat's journey as you tell the story. Ask each child to place their pencil at the beginning of the dotted line at the top of the stairs, and to move along the line as you tell the story. Check that they are using a correct pencil hold (see page 14).
■ Make up a simple story about the cat creeping down the stairs, through the sitting room, out of the cat flap and into the garden. At the start of each new picture, tell the children where to place their pencils to begin their journey.
■ Ask younger children to trace the cat's footsteps using their fingers, rather than a pencil.
■ Allow older children to find the starting-point on each picture for themselves.

More ideas
■ Use dominoes for building play, encouraging the children to build tall towers and to balance dominoes on top of each other.
■ Provide long laces and a selection of beads or cotton reels, and ask the children to 'thread a snake'. Provide eyes and tongues cut from self-adhesive paper to add to the finished snakes.

Home links
Explain to parents and carers the importance of providing the children with pencils, colouring crayons and paper. Ask them to encourage their children in drawing, colouring and cutting activities whenever possible.

Other curriculum areas
MD Set out a sequence of coloured pegs on a pegboard and ask the children to copy the sequence.
CD Draw simple outline pictures on cards and pierce holes at intervals. Use these for 'sewing' activities, using blunt needles and wool.
PSED Involve the children in preparing and passing around drinks and sandwiches for the group, thereby encouraging pouring, spreading and cutting activities.

Jigsaw pairs

What to do

■ Explain to the children that they are going to make their own jigsaws.

■ Ask each child to choose a picture for a jigsaw. Give the children pieces of card big enough for them to paste their pictures on. Show them how to spread the card thinly with glue, then ask them to place the pictures on to the card.

■ Let each child cut around the outside of their picture to remove any surplus card.

■ Now explain to the children that they are going to cut their picture in two to make the puzzle. Explain that they should try not to cut in a straight line, but should make curved or zigzag cuts.

■ When the jigsaws have been made, jumble the pieces on the table. Ask each child to pick up a piece of puzzle (not one of their own) and to try to find the matching piece.

■ Make sure that left-handed scissors are provided for left-handers.

■ Let younger children make straight cuts and draw a guideline for cutting.

■ Ask older children to cut their pictures into three pieces.

More ideas

■ Cut fish shapes from coloured paper and fit paper clips to the front end. Use plant sticks, string and a magnet to make fishing lines. Ask the children to state the colour fish that they want to catch, and then to try to 'hook' it.

Other curriculum areas

KUW Make sweets for special occasions. Check for any food allergies or dietary requirements. Show the children how to roll out marzipan or fondant icing, flavoured with peppermint essence. Let them use small cutters to shape sweets, then dip half of these into melted chocolate. Leave to dry on greaseproof paper.

CD Provide brushes of varying thicknesses for painting activities, encouraging the children to use finer brushes for detail.

Stepping Stone
Use one-handed tools and equipment.

Early Learning Goal
Use a pencil and hold it effectively to form recognisable letters, most of which are correctly formed.

Group size
Four to six children.

What you need
A selection of pictures of clear, simple images, cut from old magazines; thin card; glue; glue brushes; scissors; table.

Home links
Encourage parents and carers to create opportunities for their children to try using tools safely. Explain how they can give them bits of wood with nails partly knocked in, to practise hammering. Suggest that they provide a bucket of water and a large brush for the children to 'paint' an outside wall.

Racing cars

What to do
- Stand the children in a circle and ask them all to turn so that they are ready to move in the same direction.
- Explain that they are going to pretend to be racing cars. Tell them that they must start moving around in a circle, all at the same speed, when you say, 'Go!'. Explain that you will keep saying 'Vroom, vroom!' to help them to stay at the same speed.
- Tell them to listen very carefully. Say that when you call out, 'EEK!' they must slow down and stop, then turn around and begin to go in the opposite direction.
- Begin the game saying, 'Vroom, vroom!' in a steady rhythm so that the children move at the same pace, without bumping into one another.
- With younger children, take your place in the circle to keep the correct pace and to model the change of direction for them.
- Vary the speed of movement with older children, calling, 'EEK!' more frequently so that they change direction more often.

More ideas
- Provide the children with water pistols. Stand them about a metre from an outside wall and challenge them to use the water pistol to 'draw' a really good circle on the wall.
- Tie ribbons to the ends of sticks or rulers and show the children how to form ribbon circles in the air.

Other curriculum areas

PD Seat pairs of children opposite each other on the floor, with their legs splayed open. Leave a space of about a metre between one child's feet and the other's. Ask the children to roll a small ball back and forwards between them in a straight line.

PSED Stand the children in a circle, all facing inwards, with arms around the waists of the people beside them. Choose a child to be the 'sharer'. The children move in a circle with side-steps, until the sharer calls, 'Share!'. They then stop, while that child tells everyone what they enjoys doing most in the group.

Circle pictures

What to do

■ Explain to the children that they are going to paint a picture using circles. Put on aprons.

■ Ask the children to paint a yellow circle near the top of the paper. Next, tell them to paint two black circles at the bottom of the paper, to one side. These two circles should be a short space apart. Towards the other side of the paper, tell them to paint a red circle a little way up.

■ Explain that they are now going to turn these circles into a picture. Tell them that the yellow circle is meant to be the sun. Ask them to add to it to make it look like the sun.

■ Now ask the children to change the red circle into a flower, by adding petals, a stem and leaves.

■ Finally, explain that the two black circles are wheels. Ask them to add something to change them into a car, a bike or any vehicle they like.

■ Give younger children explicit instructions about what to do to change the circles saying, for example, 'Add some rays of sunshine to make the yellow circle into the sun'.

■ Let older children decide what they want to change their circles into.

More ideas

■ Take a page of newsprint and draw small ladybirds hidden among the print, or use small animal stickers. Ask the children to hunt for all the hidden creatures, and to circle them in pencil when they find them.

■ Make circle and line designs in sand, using a small rake, and ask the children to copy them.

Other curriculum areas

PD See how many different ways the children can find to make a skipping rope 'snake' move, for example, by moving their hands sideways and back, up and down, or in circles.

MD Play 'Guess the shape'. Pair up the children and ask them to draw a large shape with their finger on each other's backs. Their partners must guess which shape has been drawn on their backs.

Maze master

Stepping Stone
Manipulate objects with increasing control.

Early Learning Goal
Use a pencil and hold it effectively to form recognisable letters, most of which are correctly formed.

Group size
Four children.

What you need
Four sheets of A3 card; lolly sticks or pipe-cleaners; glue; four small toy vehicles.

Preparation
Glue the lolly sticks or pipe-cleaners to the sheets of card to create a series of 'roads' with different twists and turns. Pipe-cleaners will allow you to make roads with bends rather than sharp corners. Make the roads 5cm wider than the wheel span of the toy cars to be used. Draw an arrow on the card to show the entrance to the maze.

What to do
■ Explain to the children that they are going to show you how well they can 'drive' some toy cars through a maze of roads.
■ Give each child a maze and a toy vehicle. Ask the children to each place their vehicle on the arrow. Tell them that they should push their vehicle along the road and out of the maze. Explain that they must try not to touch the edges of the road with the wheels as they move the vehicle along.
■ Talk about how difficult the task was, and whether they succeeded in not touching the road sides.
■ For younger children, use larger vehicles and draw wider pathways in chalk on the ground.
■ With older children, use narrower mazes with smaller toy vehicles and provide a more complex route with a number of road mazes side by side, with road exits and entrances close to each other.

More ideas
■ Provide a variety of substances such as sand, sugar, water and flour, together with different-sized spoons, lollipop sticks and so on. Ask the children to move the substances from one container to another, experimenting with different tools.
■ Encourage play with miniature worlds such as toy farms.

Home links
Explain to parents and carers how they can help their children to practise fine movements by encouraging them to do jigsaws and to play with construction toys such as DUPLO and LEGO.

Other curriculum areas
MD Invite the children to pick up a pinch of rice and to count how many grains are in their pinch. Provide them with a matchbox and a collection of small buttons, and ask them to count how many buttons they can fit in the box.
CD Provide the children with drums, boxes or canisters. Beat different rhythms and encourage the children to copy them.

Help me home

What to do
■ Give each child a copy of the photocopiable sheet and a pencil. Explain that they are going to help each of the animals to find their way home by drawing a line along the pathways for the animals to follow. Point out the dotted line, telling the children that this shows them how to begin drawing the line along the path.
■ Say that before they begin you will help them to practise the pattern that they need to draw. Model the pattern of the first pathway by making large movements in the air. Invite the children to copy you. Do this before they begin work on each pathway.
■ Help younger children to practise each pattern in a large format, on a blank piece of paper, before working on the tracks. Guide their hands if necessary.
■ Set older children the goal of keeping their lines in the middle of the pathways.

More ideas
■ Organise a 'penny challenge'. Line up a row of penny coins on a table and ask the children to turn over all the coins, one by one, as fast as they can. Time each child and see if they can be faster the second time around.
■ Challenge the children to line up a row of dominoes, each close to the next, to demonstrate the 'domino theory'. Show them that if they push the first one over, the others will topple, too. Let them balance the dominoes on their long sides first, and then on the short sides as they become more skilful.

Other curriculum areas
PSED Provide opportunities for the children to play simple board games together, which require them to roll dice and move playing pieces.
MD Make a collection of various containers with different-sized lids. Ask the children to find and fit the correct lid for each container.

Stepping Stone
Manipulate objects with increasing control.

Early Learning Goal
Use a pencil and hold it effectively to form recognisable letters, most of which are correctly formed.

Group size
Four to six children.

What you need
A copy of the photocopiable sheet 'Follow the paths home' on page 93 for each child; pencils.

Home links
Provide a recipe for parents and carers to make play dough for their children. Explain that modelling activities with materials such as this can help the children to develop the fine finger movements that they need for writing.

Sail away

Stepping Stone
Begin to use anticlockwise movement and retrace vertical lines.

Early Learning Goal
Use a pencil and hold it effectively to form recognisable letters, most of which are correctly formed.

Group size
Four children.

What you need
A copy of the photocopiable sheet 'Finish the picture' on page 94 for each child; pencils.

What to do
■ Make sure that the children are all seated comfortably. Give each child a pencil and check that they are holding it in the correct way (see page 14).
■ Tell the children that the lines on the picture have not been drawn very clearly, and that you want them to make the picture clearer by drawing over the dotted lines. Show them the arrows at the beginning of each line and explain that they should start at the arrow each time.
■ Suggest that they may need to pause and lift the pencil sometimes on the longer patterns, if their hand is beginning to get tired.
■ When they have completed all the patterns, suggest that they draw themselves and a friend in the two portholes.
■ For younger children, paper-clip a sheet of acetate over the picture. Let them use wipe-clean coloured pens, which move over acetate more easily than a pencil on paper. Allow the children to practise several times before they try using a pencil on the paper.

■ Ask older children to make up a drawing of a face using some of the same patterns. Suggest that zigzags make good teeth, circles make good eyes, and that some of the other patterns would be good for hair.

More ideas
■ Use patterns to decorate greetings cards such as Mother's Day cards, or to form frames around paintings.
■ Roll out Plasticine tiles and let the children decorate them with patterns, using a blunt pencil.

Home links
Encourage parents and carers to involve their children in cooking activities and to suggest that they decorate home-made cards for relatives and friends.

Other curriculum areas
MD Create opportunities for the children to use tally marks for counting. For example, you could carry out a pet survey to find the most popular pet.

KUW Involve the children in cooking activities. Invite each child to mix ingredients, using stirring movements, and to practise skills such as rolling pastry.

Caterpillar curves

Early Learning Goal
Use a pencil and hold it effectively to form recognisable letters, most of which are correctly formed.

Group size
Four children.

What you need
A copy of the photocopiable sheets 'Write the letters' on pages 95 and 96 for each child, plus one spare; pencils.

What to do

■ Make sure that the children are seated comfortably.

■ Explain to the children that they are going to write some letters. Tell them that 'Curvy Caterpillar' is going to help them by curling into the shape of different letters. Say that they are going to draw the stripe on his body first to make the shape of the letter.

■ Give each child a pencil and check that they are holding it in the correct way (see page 14).

■ Explain that they must always start at Curvy Caterpillar's head and end at his tail. Demonstrate this on the spare photocopiable sheet for each new letter shape.

■ As the children write each letter, check that they are holding the pencil correctly and forming the letter shape correctly.

■ Help younger children to develop a correct pencil hold by providing pencil grips, and enlarge the photocopiable sheet if necessary.

■ Ask older children to practise each letter shape on a blank piece of paper when they have completed the task.

More ideas

■ Show the children how to bend and cut pipe-cleaners to make different letters. Glue the 'letters' on to cards to use as tactile reminders of letter shapes. Glue a picture of an object with the corresponding initial letter on to the reverse of the card

■ Fill a baking tray with salt or sand and use it to practise writing letter shapes.

Home links
Ask parents and carers to encourage their children to 'sign' cards and notes to family and friends, using at least the initial letter of their name.

Other curriculum areas

KUW ■ Make an alphabet snake. Ask the children to write large letters on 10cm square pieces of card in felt-tipped pen (provide a faint pencil guideline). Cut a snake's head and tail from card. Use the letters to build a large alphabet snake on the floor.

CD ■ Ask the children to 'draw' the initial letter of their name on paper using a glue stick. Sprinkle the letter with glitter.

The 'I can' tree

Early Learning Goal
Use a pencil and hold it effectively to form recognisable letters, most of which are correctly formed.

Group size
Four to six children.

What you need
A sheet of A3 paper and several leaf-shaped pieces of paper for each child; pencils; glue; glue brushes.

Preparation
Draw an outline tree trunk and branches on each A3 sheet, allowing room for leaves to be added to the branches. Cut leaf-shaped pieces of paper. Make these large enough to allow for child-sized writing.

Home links
Ask parents and carers to make sure that materials for writing activities are available for their children. Explain the importance of responding with praise to any attempt at writing.

What to do
■ Explain to the children that they are going to make an 'I can' tree to show everyone all the things that they can do.
■ Give each child a tree outline and a 'leaf'. Tell them that they are going to write 'I can' on the leaf and then add something that they can do. Write 'I can' on a piece of paper in large letters as a model for the children. Ask them to write this.
■ Now talk about simple things that they can do such as run, hop, skip, jump and swim. Ask each child to choose one of these words to write on their leaf. Help them to work out the letters that they need to write.
■ Invite each child to glue their finished leaf to a branch of the tree and then to start another leaf.
■ Encourage younger children to simply copy 'I can', and write the words that they suggest for them.
■ Let older children attempt their achievement words for themselves.

More ideas
■ Provide the children with acetate sheets and wipe-clean pens to trace letter shapes for extra practice.
■ Make a group 'We like' tree using heart-shaped pieces of paper as fruit on the tree.

Other curriculum areas
PD Ask the children to curl their bodies into particular letter shapes, working together in pairs or threes, if necessary.

KUW Let the children watch the initial letters of their names 'grow'. Ask them to draw it in felt-tipped pen on a piece of kitchen roll, then place this on a tray and dampen it slightly. Tell them to sprinkle cress seeds along the letter shape and then keep the paper damp.

Speaking and listening (1)

Name _____

Goals	Assessment	Date
Language for communication		
Interact with others, negotiating plans and activities and taking turns in conversation.		
Enjoy listening to and using spoken and written language, and readily turn to it in their play and learning.		
Sustain attentive listening, responding to what they have heard by relevant comments, questions or actions.		
Listen with enjoyment, and respond to stories, songs and other music, rhymes and poems and make up their own stories, songs, rhymes and poems.		
Extend their vocabulary, exploring the meanings and sounds of new words.		
Speak clearly and audibly with confidence and control and show awareness of the listener, for example by their use of conventions such as greetings, 'please' and 'thank you'.		

Speaking and listening (2)

Name _____

Goals	Assessment	Date
Language for thinking		
Use language to imagine and re-create roles and experiences.		
Use talk to organise, sequence and clarify thinking, ideas, feelings and events.		
Linking sounds and letters		
Hear and say initial and final sounds in words, and short vowel sounds within words.		
Link sounds to letters, naming and sounding the letters of the alphabet.		
Use their phonic knowledge to write simple regular words and make phonetically plausible attempts at more complex words.		

Reading

Name _____

Goals	Assessment	Date
Reading		
Explore and experiment with sounds, words and texts.		
Retell narratives in the correct sequence, drawing on language patterns of stories.		
Read a range of familiar and common words and simple sentences independently.		
Know that print carries meaning and, in English, is read from left to right and top to bottom.		
Show an understanding of the elements of stories, such as main character, sequence of events, and openings, and how information can be found in non-fiction texts to answer questions about where, who, why and how.		

Writing and handwriting

Name _____

Goals	Assessment	Date
Writing		
Use their phonic knowledge to write simple regular words and make phonetically plausible attempts at more complex words.		
Attempt writing for different purposes, using features of different forms such as lists, stories and instructions.		
Write their own names and other things such as labels and captions and begin to form simple sentences, sometimes using punctuation.		
Handwriting		
Use a pencil and hold it effectively to form recognisable letters, most of which are correctly formed.		

Photocopiable

Communication, language and literacy

Let's dress Bear

The same sound?

Photocopiable   Communication, language and literacy

Say the sounds

Follow the alphabet

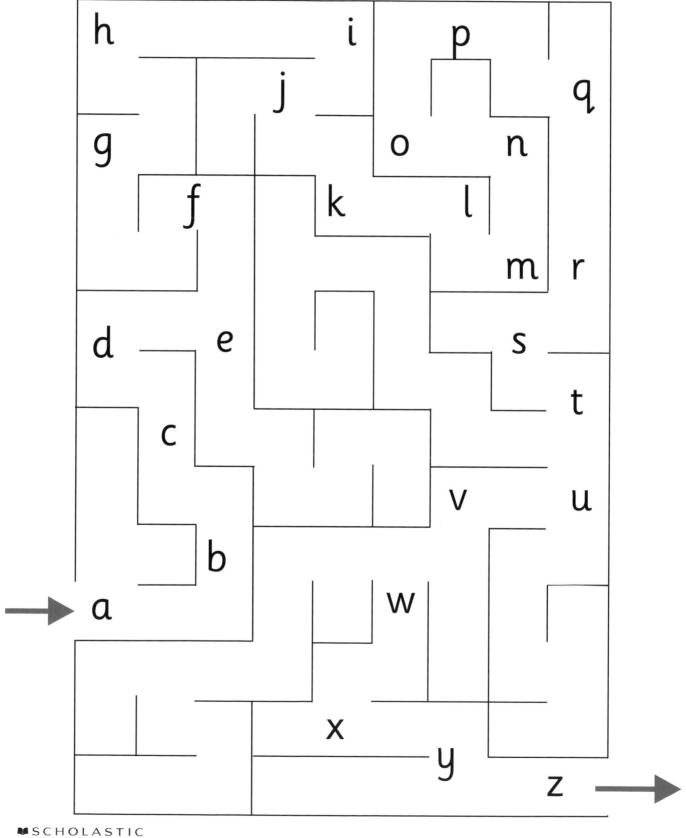

Photocopiable

Communication, language and literacy

Make new words

Find the rhyme

rug   cap   pan

Photocopiable   Communication, language and literacy

What's that noise?

Cornflake cookies

Ingredients
For four people
2 x 225g bars of chocolate (melted)
4 cupfuls of cornflakes
paper cake cases

Optional special ingredients
4 tablespoons of raisins
or
4 tablespoons of chopped dried apricots

What to do

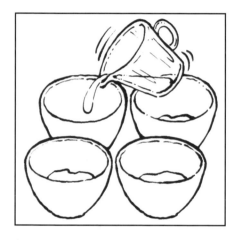

I Share the melted chocolate between four bowls.

2 Add one cup of cornflakes to each bowl. (Add special ingredient.)

3 Stir gently until mixed.

4 Place spoonfuls of mixture into paper cake cases.

5 Leave to set.

Word detectives

The hat is big. ☐

The rat is big. ☐

The cat is on the box. ☐

The cat is in the box. ☐

A cat is on the bed. ☐

A can is on the bed. ☐

Pat has a dog. ☐

Pat has a bag. ☐

Let's go exploring!

Photocopiable

Communication, language and literacy

Follow the paths home

Finish the picture

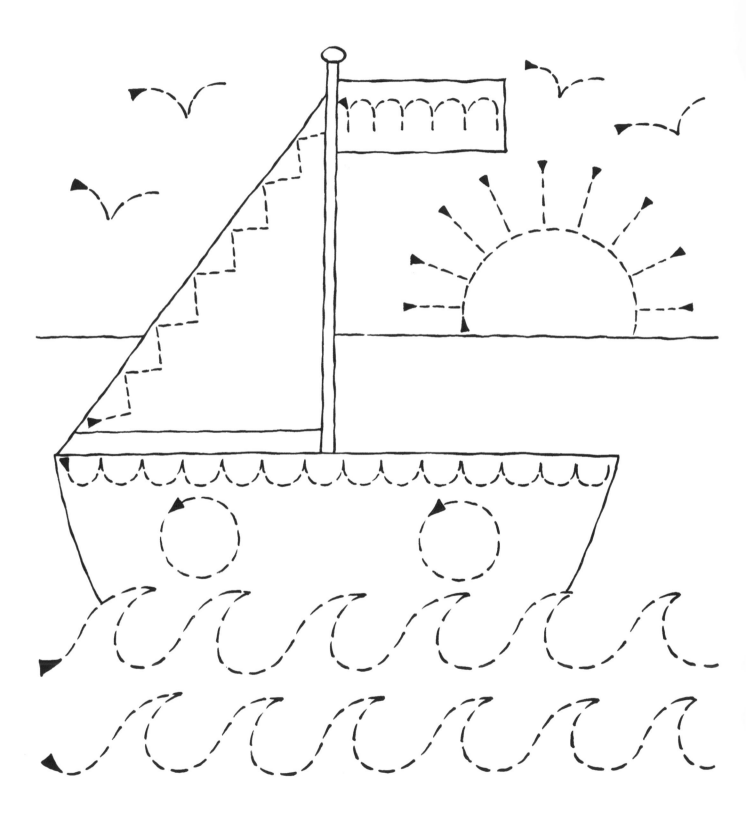

Photocopiable   **Communication, language and literacy**

Write the letters (1)

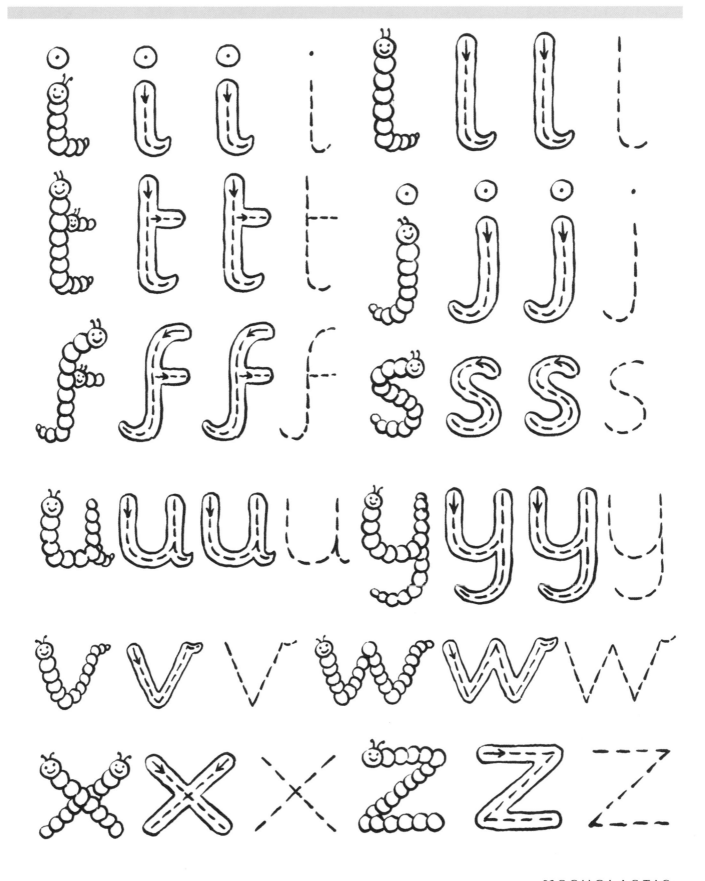

Write the letters (2)

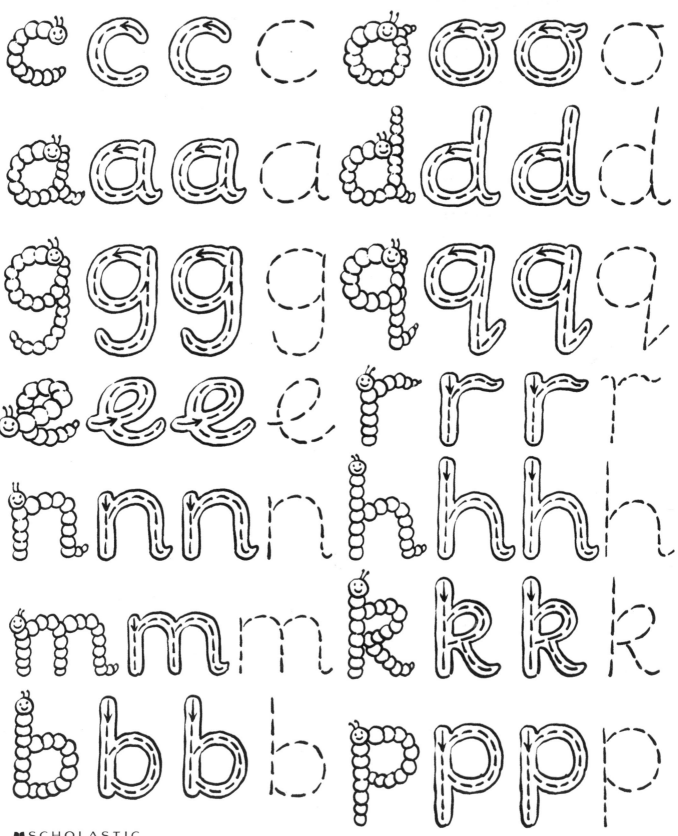

Communication, language and literacy